EYES
OF THE
HEART

EYES
OF THE
HEART

SEEING GOD
IN AN AGE
OF SCIENCE

RUSSELL
HAITCH

FORTRESS PRESS
MINNEAPOLIS

EYES OF THE HEART
Seeing God in an Age of Science

Cover Image: DrRave/istockphoto.com; parys/istockphoto.com
Cover Design: Brad Norr Design

Print ISBN: 978-1-5064-5054-4
Ebook ISBN: 978-1-5064-5055-1

For my parents,
whose arguments about God got me thinking

CONTENTS

Just a Glass of Water

You sit down at a restaurant and ask for a glass of water. Your server brings it over and says, "Careful. This glass contains water molecules that Jesus and his disciples drank at the Last Supper."

She isn't kidding. Your server is a Christian but also a scientist who knows her facts. And the facts in this case look more interesting than anything on the menu.

Molecules are incredibly small, so a single glass of water contains a staggering number of them. By comparison, if you took all the water in world—all five oceans plus all the lakes, rivers, streams, icecaps, and groundwater on earth—and poured it all into separate twelve-ounce containers, you would obviously have a large number of tumblers. But not as large as the number of molecules in just one glass of water.

Over time, molecules disperse, mixing with all the other water out there. And so it comes to pass, after two thousand years of mixing, you can be pretty sure the next water you drink will contain at least a few molecules that Jesus also drank. Why go all the way to Jerusalem to walk in the footsteps of Jesus when you can simply go to the kitchen, turn on the tap, and drink water (at least a few molecules) that once touched his very lips?

After supper has ended, your server takes this idea further. Blood, she points out, is mainly water. Which means that every day, people around the world are drinking molecules that were once the blood of Christ—not as a spiritual act but a scientific fact. Two atoms of hydrogen plus one atom of oxygen (H_2O) equals one molecule of water, and molecules are small beyond belief.[1]

We can think of blood, water, or anything else in smaller and smaller quantities, smaller even than molecules and atoms, smaller than protons, gluons, or quarks. We are moving in a direction called the Little Infinity.

The Little Infinity, so far as we know, is mostly empty space. The nucleus of an atom vibrating inside its surrounding electrons is like a fly buzzing inside an empty football stadium. Nuclear interactions hold atoms together, but still, a wall of "solid" granite is mostly empty space, from the atomic point of view. If you walked smack into a stone wall, over and over, eventually your body could pass right through it, just like Jesus in the Gospels passing through walls to the Upper Room after his resurrection. Unlike Jesus, you would need to walk into the same stone wall for billions or trillions of years before all the atoms aligned just right.[2] Or possibly you could get lucky on the first try.

Through the eyes of science, the entire world down to the Little Infinity is an amazing, coruscating wonderland.

Go the other direction, toward the Big Infinity, and the scale is equally wonderful and impossible to fathom. Our pale blue dot of a planet orbits an average star, and how many other stars are out there? Even if we know the answer, we cannot really grasp the magnitude. Pretend a grain of sand along the beach represents one star. In the known universe, there are more stars than all the grains of sand on all the beaches of all the oceans on Earth.[3] That tells us their number but not their size. The sun is large

---

[1] Many scientists believe water molecules are extremely stable, even over millions of years. Charles Fishman claims that much of the water we now drink was once dinosaur urine. See *The Big Thirst* (New York: Simon and Schuster, 2011). But "stable" cannot mean static. The physical universe is always in flux, including the infinitesimal parts of a molecule: as some electrons of a hydrogen atom get sucked away, other electrons enter and become bonded to the atom's protons. So is the water molecule really the same over time, since it may or may not have identical physical stuff? It's hard to say, but if I can speak of myself as having the same body I did one minute ago—even though a million cells in my body are dying every second—then it also makes sense to say we are drinking some of the same molecules that were once in the blood of Jesus. My thanks to Dr. Isaac Ottoni Wilhelm for help with this clarification.

[2] Brian Greene, *The Elegant Universe* (New York: Random House, 1999), 116.

[3] The number of stars in the visible universe is estimated to be between 10^{22} and 10^{24}, so if the entire earth's surface were covered with a one-meter-deep layer of sand grains that were one

enough to hold 1.3 million Earths, and some stars are eighteen hundred times larger than the sun. That tells us their size but not their speed. Stars are not idly twinkling but rather hurtling through space at speeds up to two million miles an hour, emitting the energy of a hundred billion nuclear bombs every second.

Yet the Big Infinity, so far as we know, is mainly dusty space. Despite their incredible size, stars are just puny specks compared with the dark and empty spaces between them. In our galaxy, the typical distance between any two stars is thirty *trillion* miles. Our galaxy is relatively crowded. Overall in the known universe, the average distance between two stars is ten thousand trillion miles.[4]

"The eternal silence of these infinite spaces terrifies me" is how Blaise Pascal once put it.[5]

Pascal's reaction is not unusual. Among believers today, 45 percent say they "often feel a sense of wonder about the universe." Among atheists, the number is 54 percent.[6] For believers and atheists alike, the universe is a wonderland, and seeing it through the eyes of science increases our sense of awe. Imagine—molecules so small that people every day are drinking the physical substance of Christ's blood. A universe so big that the sun becomes a speck and the earth recedes to nothing. And all that empty space between stars or within the atom—is it all empty of meaning, too?

Teenage years are typically when we start to ask these sorts of questions in an acute way. Coming to a sense of themselves and the universe, young people are apt to wonder, Where is it all headed? What does it all add up to? What does any of it mean? Christian parents, teachers,

---

millimeter in diameter, there would be about 2×10^{23} grains of sand. Since beaches do not cover the entire planet, it's safe to estimate that stars outnumber sand grains. My thanks to Professor Jonathan Frye for this and subsequent calculations.

[4] If the volume of the visible universe is 4×10^{80} meters squared and the number of stars is 10^{23}, then the average volume of space per star is 4×10^{57} meters squared, and the average distance between stars would be the cube root of that number, or approximately 1.6×10^{19} meters. At about 1,600 meters per mile, that equals 10^{16} miles.

[5] Blaise Pascal, *Pensées* (New York: E. P. Dutton, 1958), 61.

[6] David Masci and Michael Lipka, "Americans May Be Getting Less Religious, but Feelings of Spirituality Are on the Rise," Pew Research Center, January 21, 2016, https://tinyurl.com/y9hw5dzz.

and ministers hope their youth will decide that it all points to God. It all coheres around Jesus Christ (Col 1:17), who fills the cosmos with radiant purpose.

Yet this faithful outcome is far from certain. Consider the case of the world's most famous atheist.

Richard Dawkins and I attended the same boarding school in England, though in different decades. I went back one year to talk to a group of Sixth Form students about the poetry of Robert Frost. He returned to tell a much larger group about evolution and his journey to atheism. Some of what he said can be found in his book *The God Delusion*.[7] There Dawkins recalls the school chaplain from his time as a young schoolboy. The chaplain, when he himself was a boy, had a mystical experience in nature one afternoon as he "lay prone in the grass" and "suddenly found himself overwhelmed by a heightened awareness" of roots and stems, ants and beetles and billions of unseen bacteria—his mind moving in the direction of the Little Infinity. One wonder led to another, and this boy grew up to become an Anglican priest.

Dawkins reports that he, as a young boy living with his British parents in Kenya, also had a "quasi-mystical response to nature and the universe" when at night he looked up at "the stars, dazzled by Orion, Cassiopeia and Ursa Minor, tearful with the unheard music of the Milky Way"—his mind moving in the direction of the Big Infinity. One wonder led to another, and this boy grew up to become the world's most famous atheist.

The future priest and budding atheist were both awestruck by the wonders of nature but over time came to see life differently. When two roads diverged in a yellow wood, they took different routes to knowing reality. An increasing number of young people today are taking Dawkins's route. Modern scientific thinking, along with other forces, is training their minds to focus on the physical world. As a result, their faith in God may grow fainter or fade away entirely.

We don't want to ignore this problem. We cannot skirt past differences between faith and science. Faith and science are indeed different ways of

---

[7] Richard Dawkins, *The God Delusion* (New York: Houghton Mifflin, 2006), 31–32.

knowing reality. They rely on different premises, procedures, and proofs. These differences matter.

But these differences do not need to spell division. Starting in childhood, we can grow to see reality using the eyes of science but also, even more so, a different set of "eyes," which the Bible calls the "eyes of the heart." Faith and science can be complementary, not competing. We can come to a fuller, higher vision of reality by having both sets of eyes.

The purpose of this book is to offer a model for seeing reality this way. The second half of the book then tests this model by looking at issues of evolution and creation, an area that has generated a lot of passion over the years.

Scientists and believers are both passionate about their convictions. Thankfully, the model offered in this book does not require either group to tamp down, weaken, or compromise their passion and conviction. As the reader, you may decide to do some rethinking, but you will not need a pair of scissors. You will not be asked to cut out parts of the Bible or even chapters of science textbooks. If your convictions lead you to delete a chapter or two of this book, that's okay. Hopefully, you will find enough value in the remaining pages to repay your time and attention.

Speaking of convictions, let me say a word about my own. I traveled a hard road away from faith in adolescence and back to faith in young adulthood. I have walked alongside both the atheist and the priest. I think this journey has enabled me to relate to people of different faiths or no religious faith. But today, my convictions are decidedly Christian.

"What kind of Christian?" you may ask. It's a fair question. Like you, perhaps, I have been influenced by parents and friends. My mother grew up Anglican, but years of intense personal study led her to become Eastern Orthodox. My father grew up Lutheran (and I too was baptized in a Lutheran church), but as an adult he developed a sturdy Baptist theology that served him well through years of prison ministry. Perhaps splitting the difference between mother and father, I eventually became a Methodist pastor, yet I went on to teach for both Reformed and Anabaptist seminaries. Over the years, I have served in pastoral and teaching positions with people across the theological spectrum, from the most fundamentally conservative to the most radically progressive. Probably most of my best friends over these same years have been Pentecostal or Roman Catholic. My wife, when asked recently to describe herself, replied, "Can't I just be a Christian?"

I think God has used all these influences and still God is greater than all these influences. If, after reading this book, you can think of a good label for me, please write to inform me. It might be helpful for my obituary, if not my afterlife.

Let me also say a word about this book's intended "audience." No scientific background is needed. I am not a scientist but a pastor and teacher—a theologian, if you will. Professional scientists have reviewed portions of this book (if there are still errors, I hope they are not fatal), but the book's intended audience is not scientists; it is all of us who live in an "age of science." More specifically, I initially had in mind an audience of youth ministers, both paid and volunteer. I thought of college students and seminarians in training for ministry. I recalled my own years of youth ministry and how I wished I had been better prepared for the questions of young people regarding science. The research I read suggested other ministers felt the same way. Only 1 percent of youth pastors say they have addressed any science-related subject in the last year. Yet half of 13- to 17-year-olds say they want to pursue a science-related career. This gap is what got me started on this project.[8]

As I continued working on the book, I was struck by something social scientists were reporting about parents. Most parents see themselves—not the pastor or youth pastor—as having the primary responsibility for their children's spiritual development.[9] I knew that was certainly true for my wife and me. So I continued writing and rewriting with an audience of parents also in mind.

---

[8] Jean M. Twenge, *iGen: Why Today's Super-Connected Kids Are Growing Up Less Rebellious, More Tolerant, Less Happy—and Completely Unprepared for Adulthood* (New York, NY: Atria Books, 2017), 139. Cf. David Kinnamon, *You Lost Me: Why Young Christians Are Leaving The Church . . . and Rethinking Faith* (Grand Rapids, MI: Baker Books, 2016).
[9] Christian Smith, Bridget Ritz, and Michael Rotolo, *Religious Parenting: Transmitting Religious Faith and Values in Contemporary America* (Princeton, NJ: Princeton University Press, 2020).

The entire process put me more closely in touch with my own growing-up years. I recalled reading the Bible or books on faith and thinking, "But what about science?" I remembered learning about science in school and then asking myself, "But where is God in all this?" So I tried to write the kind of book that I might have wanted to read when I was a teenager or in college.

Speaking to an audience this broad on a topic this big seems ambitious. But I think my real ambition is to inspire a few people, of any age or occupation, to grow in grace and knowledge. My hope—I could even call it a promise—is this: in the following pages, you will encounter some ideas that are ancient enough to feel new as well as some new ideas that are cogent enough to be true.

As I write these words, the world is struggling through a pandemic with no end in sight. We are looking to science to give us light. Thank God for scientists! Perhaps by the time you read these words, a clear way forward will have been found; perhaps not. But one thing is certain. Though science can help us solve many problems of life, it cannot answer the question of life itself. Science cannot tell us why we live. It cannot supply the love we need to make life worthwhile. It cannot connect us to a personal power greater than ourselves. Without all this—without a spiritual order to life—we too easily lurch from one anxiety to another.

More than ever, young and old together need to rediscover another way of seeing. Through eyes of the heart, we are able to see, gradually or suddenly, God's love spanning the universe, from the Big Infinity to the Little Infinity. And we are able to sense this same love reaching deeply into the center of our lives.

PART I

FAITH AND SCIENCE

CHAPTER 1

Opportunity Knocks

And you, of tender years,
Can't know the fears that your elders grew by.
—Crosby, Stills & Nash,
"Teach Your Children Well"

The goal of this book is to help youth see reality through eyes of both faith and science. Though we live in an age of science, and though technology courses through our cultural bloodstream, still most parents and pastors will shy away from topics in which science and faith converge. Many of us feel inadequate to the task. We may recall a failed chemistry exam or some other proof of our scientific ineptitude. We may also harbor fears that faith is bound to lose some ground any time it interacts with science. Youth ministers, charged with protecting the tender faith of their young flock, have an especially hard time seeing how discussions of science are going to help young people have *fewer* doubts.

For many problems and temptations of adolescence, avoidance is a fine strategy. As my mother used to say, "Just wait; they'll grow out of it." But this strategy will not work with issues of faith and science. If there are doubts, they will deepen over time, and where there are conflicts, the rifts will widen, and the gravitational pull for youth will be toward a secular culture and naturalistic worldview, which science is purported to support.

Even when youth are not formally studying science subjects in school, a scientific, technological, and naturalistic sense of reality pervades their lives. Young people learn to trust science implicitly, through the medicines they take and the devices affixed to their fingertips. They trust scientists. The "scientific community" inspires twice as much public confidence as "organized religion."[1] In the United States, science is indisputably our public truth. If we want youth to see their faith convictions as something more than just private opinions, then we need to help them think through the relationship between Spirit and science.

In facing our fears, we encounter opportunity. Youth can grow more deeply into their faith when they are able to integrate it with the science and technology that govern daily life. This book is structured in terms of opportunity, obstacles, and solution.

First, we have a beautiful opportunity to tell youth about intersections and harmonies between faith and science. Without presuming to put faith and science on the same plane or equal footing, we can explain how faith and science are allies in our seeing the amplitude of God's reality. Both often begin in wonder, and though they proceed along different lines, the two endeavors can complement and even correct each other. The scientific impulse to observe, inspect, and test is found within the Bible. After healing a leper, Jesus tells him, "Go, show yourself to the priest." The priest was supposed to examine the evidence and verify that a healing had taken place.

In seizing this opportunity, we encounter obstacles. Though faith and science were once conjoined in Christian history—including in the early modern period, when natural theology and natural science were partners—today theology and science have drifted apart and sometimes been wrenched apart. Former allies are now portrayed as foes. The topic of human origins comes to mind. Issues of creation and evolution continue to vex many young people.

Perusing popular media, we now and then see other ways that science and faith get pitted against each other. For instance, the new governor of Wisconsin proclaimed in 2019 that the seasonal tree in the state capitol building would be called a holiday tree rather than a Christmas tree—and he took one step further. Announcing the theme of "Celebrate Science," he asked schoolchildren to "submit science-related ornaments to adorn

---

[1] Mark Chaves, *American Religion: Contemporary Trends* (Princeton, NJ: Princeton University Press, 2011), 77.

the tree."[2] The copresident of the Freedom from Religion Foundation applauded this move as being "more inclusive." While not an earth-shaking story, still it conveys how science is considered public truth, and it fuels the notion that to be pro-science is to be anti-Christian, or at least anti-Christmas. However, this sort of conflict is not the worst problem youth ministers face with regard to faith and science.

Where there is conflict, it means there is some kind of relationship, along with the hope of reaching resolution. This book takes the position that the bigger problem is not conflict but non-interaction. The divorce between faith and science means that people struggle to live integrated lives in two parallel universes—the Sunday universe of faith, the Monday universe of science and technology. Though young people may see threads of faith and science closely connected on digital feeds, there is a mental chasm between their disparate thought worlds. Both science and Christianity claim to be true. Yet they arrive at their truths by starting from different premises, relying on different procedures, and arriving at different proofs.

In short, we are caught between two kinds of obstacles. Conflict and non-interaction are the Scylla and Charybdis of our attempts to help youth relate faith and science.

As a solution to the problems of both conflictual interaction and non-interaction, I propose a model that takes us back to the person of Jesus and a method that hopefully scientists and ministers alike will find fair-minded. This solution is not meant to be a cure-all but rather a road in the right direction. To test this approach, I will offer a reading of Genesis and Romans that unlocks hidden meaning and resolves antagonism with modern science. In the process, we will discover content to teach youth about two topics of supreme importance in Christianity—namely, life and death.

The need for this kind of teaching becomes obvious if we look again at recent social science research. In a national study, about 80 percent of American teens said they were Christians, but only about 8 percent were described by researcher Kenda Creasy Dean as being "highly devoted."

---

[2] "Scott Walker Wades into 'Holiday Tree' Fight with Menorah Tweet," CBS News, November 8, 2019, https://tinyurl.com/y3qbue2v.

These teens were more likely to be able to state clearly what they believed and demonstrate the difference those beliefs make in their lives.[3] If we want our youth to be part of the 8 percent (for their fulfillment and God's glory), then we need to address the gap between faith and science.

Overall, teens who are more receptive to mainstream science have a harder time articulating a coherent God-centered worldview, whereas teens who are more lucid about their faith have a harder time harmonizing it with mainstream science. Put another way, teens who profess a scientific worldview struggle with how God fits into it, while teens who profess a biblical worldview struggle with certain issues of science, such as the age of the universe and origins of human beings. Most youth embody both biblical and scientific sensibilities, but the two are not on speaking terms. They are being told, by strong voices on both sides, that they must choose this day whether to be modernly scientific or biblically faithful. But what about the young person who wants to be both?

That is the person for whom this book is written. In writing to parents, pastors, youth ministers, and thoughtful young people, my goal is to help us see through eyes of science but also through what the Bible calls the eyes of the heart (Eph 1:18). In this way, the universe of science can become again the cosmos of our Creator. The goal is to help young people develop a Christian frame of mind and sense of reality—a Christian feeling for how things are and what life is all about. This goal, I realize, faces two initial objections.

First, a parent or pastor may say, "Look, I'm really not too focused on what my teenagers believe. Their active minds come up with all sorts of stuff. I just want them to feel like they belong in church—that they are part of our community." It's true, a sense of belonging matters. And someone else may say, "Look, I just want them to learn some spiritual practices and habits of good behavior." It's true, behaving also matters.

---

[3] Kenda Creasy Dean, *Almost Christian: What the Faith of Our Teenagers Is Telling the American Church* (New York: Oxford University Press, 2010), 19, 46. See also Christian Smith with Melinda Lundquist Denton, *Soul Searching: The Religious and Spiritual Lives of American Teenagers* (New York: Oxford University Press, 2005).

But so too does believing. In fact, believing, belonging, and behaving are intertwined. What we believe will shape how we behave and where we belong. And "belief" does not necessarily mean a list of things that teens can stand up and recite (though creeds do have their place), but instead belief encompasses their frame of mind, their sense of reality, their intuition of what life is all about. Is the youth meeting one more activity in an overscheduled week or a joining together of the body of Christ? The answer depends on what we believe—our frame of mind and sense of reality. Is a spiritual practice one more task on the long road to self-improvement or a graceful conduit of the Holy Spirit's power? Again, the answer depends on how we think and what we believe. In short, it is worth paying attention to our frame of mind, as the following pages intend to do.

A second objection to engaging faith and science is that it may feel risky. Since science can become as divisive as politics in some church settings, it might seem prudent to say little or nothing. However, if you are silent, other voices will guide your youth in the faith-and-science discussion, and you may not be happy with what they hear. Still, I can appreciate the apprehension. Already some readers must be skeptical. Is this book going to be pushing "creation science"? Is it going to be pushing "billions of years"?

My aim is not to push anything so much as pull young people toward God at a time when science and technology seem to be pulling them away. This centrifugal force is not the fault of science and technology. Scientists have worked hard, done their job, and made good discoveries. Technologists have capitalized on those discoveries and made good money. The church has often adopted a similar mindset. Maybe there's some breakthrough discovery that will cause our church to grow or some shiny new technology we can deploy. Maybe there is. But it could be that much of what we hope to discover has already been found. Still, we would need to find it again for ourselves. In the depths of Christian tradition, we can find ways of thinking that will help youth unite faith and science and in the process draw them closer to God.

CHAPTER 2

How Science Can Help Faith and Vice Versa

L ife in the Psalms is not altogether easy. There are many enemies whose teeth we'd like to smash. But we also find moments of sublime consolation. Stand under the night sky, unpolluted by electric light, and drink in the jeweled beauty of God's handmade moon and stars (Ps 8:3). After a cold desert night, feel the sun's awakening warmth (Ps 19:6). Then think about us, humanity. Why should God care for us, given our puny size in comparison with the incredibly vast cosmos (Ps 8:4)? Yet God does care, supremely, looking favorably on us as we were formed in our mother's womb (Ps 139:13). These depictions arise from a place of observation and wonder, the same place science also begins.

Turning to Leviticus and to medical matters such as mildew and leprosy, the biblical instructions even start to sound a bit scientific. If you suspect mildew, "go and tell the priest, 'I have seen something that looks like mildew in my house'" (Lev 14:35 NIV). The priest for his part should "examine the mildew on the walls, and if it has greenish or reddish depressions that appear to be deeper than the surface of the wall," the house should be shuttered for seven days, then reexamined, and then repaired according to a set protocol. If the mildew has not spread, then the house is to be purified with the blood of a bird killed over fresh water in a clay pot (Lev 14:50).

Don't let the bird throw you; some of our present-day protocols will sound strange to people three thousand years from now. The main point is that Leviticus contains these God-given instructions to figure things out by observation ("greenish or reddish depression"), measurement ("deeper than the surface"), and testing ("for seven days"). It almost feels like a command to be scientific.

Solomon was king but also a science teacher who taught about mammals, birds, reptiles, and fish (1 Kgs 4:33). Jesus explained the deep things of God by referring to seeds, soil, flowers, birds, fish, trees, and very many sheep. People then did not see a universe divided between natural and supernatural forces but rather beheld a cosmos suffused with God's presence. The physical and spiritual dimensions were more united for them than they are for us today. It makes good biblical sense to bring faith and science back together. It also makes good historical sense.

Western science began inside the church, and for most of the past two thousand years, faith and science were conjoined. In Syria, in the seventh century, Saint Isaac taught that we have both physical eyes to see the world and spiritual eyes to see God's glory hidden in creation.[1]

In Germany, in the twelfth century, Hildegard of Bingen reported that her physical eyes were actually the means through which she received spiritual visions. She used those same eyes to study plants and other things in nature and so became the mother of science in Germany.

Across Europe, in the sixteenth century, Protestant Reformers said the "book" of nature (scientific study) reveals God when read alongside the book of Scripture.

The idea that nature and the Bible are two complementary "books" was proposed in the Latin Middle Ages. These years were once called the Dark Ages, on the assumption that people were in the dark about science and classical learning, but more recent scholarship has sought to dispel this notion by casting light on medieval progress. Rodney Stark contends that science flourished under church patronage, and along with science

---

[1] Saint Isaac, Hom. 46, *The Ascetical Homilies of St. Isaac the Syrian* (Boston: Holy Transfiguration Monastery, 2011), 223.

came new technology: eyeglasses, stirrups and saddles, chimneys, dams, water- and wind-powered mills, and selective plant breeding undertaken in monasteries by devout believers such as Hildegard of Bingen.[2]

These developments may seem rudimentary and slow, but science is cumulative. The average physics PhD today knows more than Newton, though in his day Newton was the greatest scientist who had ever lived. Likewise, you can earn a doctoral degree in evolutionary biology without reading a single page of Darwin because the field has progressed so much since his time. Science and technology also seem to follow what the inventor Ray Kurzweil has called the law of accelerating returns. The entire human genome was transcribed in fifteen years, but starting out was slow going. After the first year, they had completed only one ten-thousandth of the project. Toward the end is when the pieces fell rapidly into place.[3]

In short, the science done by believers in former centuries set the stage for the explosive growth we see today. Further, when science was accelerating during the Enlightenment, the central figures were all still religious people, such as Newton and Bacon. The vocal opponents of religion, such as Voltaire, were "literary men" and not scientists.[4]

For centuries, therefore, the church staunchly supported science, and most scientists were fervently faithful. People of science and people of faith were in full agreement because they were the same people. They saw the cosmos through both physical eyes and "eyes of the heart." The world of knowledge was not yet divided into territories called science and religion. As historian Peter Harrison recounts, *religio* and *scientia* were both internal virtues. They were complementary aspects of Christian piety long before they became separate external bodies of knowledge.[5]

The language of Western science reveals its close historic connection to Christian faith. The word *scientist* did not become popular until the

---

[2] Rodney Stark, *The Triumph of Christianity: How the Jesus Movement Became the World's Largest Religion* (New York: HarperCollins, 2012), 239–44.
[3] Ray Kurzweil, *The Singularity Is Near: When Humans Transcend Biology* (New York: Penguin, 2005), 13.
[4] Stark, *The Triumph of Christianity*, 252.
[5] Peter Harrison, *The Territories of Science and Religion* (Chicago: University of Chicago Press, 2017).

late nineteenth century. Previously, men and women who studied nature were called naturalists. The practical research of naturalism had theoretical partners called natural philosophy and natural theology. People are often surprised to learn that Darwin earned a degree in theology or that Newton wrote more theology than he did science, but these facts make perfect sense once we grasp the close-knit history of faith and science.

When Francis Bacon and others were making the case that science needed to become grounded in fieldwork and experimentation, this newer empirical approach was initially met with skepticism. Most scientists were gentlemen and thus reluctant to value work that entailed getting dirt under their fingernails. To burnish the reputation of empirical science, proponents of this newer approach described it as the suitable counterpart to natural theology, since theology was clearly a respectable pursuit. Today a few vocal scientists who double as public intellectuals portray scientific progress and religious faith as mortal enemies, but it helps to know the history of faith and science and the one-time happy marriage between them. Science was seen as a way of proving God's existence before it became seen as a way of disproving it.

The physicist and theologian John Polkinghorne has remarked that life is fuller when we have "binocular vision," an ability to see reality through eyes of both faith and science. The message we need to offer young people is not simply that you can advance in science and retain your faith. Rather, the church benefits from having good scientists. Faith and science can illuminate and complement each other. They can even help to correct each other. How so?

The answer is a central argument of this book: Science can help to correct the exaggerating tendency of faith. And faith can correct the reducing tendency of science.

Consider faith's tendency to exaggerate. When our eyes are opened to see the deep things of God, our ears are ready to believe anything. Since "nothing is impossible with God," every story of faith is potentially plausible. At the same time, we are not supposed to be gullible. A miraculous healing can build faith, but a fraudulent claim can just as quickly tear it down. Verification is actually a sound biblical principle. God's people are told to test the prophets because not all prophets actually speak for God (Deut 18:21–22). "Test the spirits" (1 John 4:1) because not all spirits come from God. Indeed, "test everything" (1 Thess 5:21).

Testing entails looking beneath the surface and probing for evidence. Think of Thomas, who heard the good news of Jesus's resurrection from people who had actually seen Jesus. Still, Thomas needed to see and touch for himself. Probably every youth group has a Thomas or two.

Jesus meets Thomas's request for empirical verification—put your finger into my nail marks, says Jesus; put your whole hand into my side—at the same time he blesses those who are able to believe without this exact evidence. Skepticism that doubts everything is a weakness, but skepticism that seeks to examine and test everything can lead to stronger faith. And in the end, tradition tells us that Thomas's faith took him farther than any other disciple, all the way to India.

Not every disciple is a Thomas, and not every Christian needs to become a scientist, but a scientific sensibility can serve to check the exaggerating tendency of faith. How many times have we listened to a sermon illustration and wondered whether it was really true? Yet we almost feel guilty for harboring the thought. If the church were more scientific, it would help us avoid the charge that we are ready to believe any malarkey. Here, sadly, the case of the Malarkeys is instructive.

Kevin and Alex Malarkey, father and son, wrote a best-selling book in which Alex offered an "eyewitness" account of heaven. His visit to heaven was said to have occurred at age six, after an auto accident. Alex's skull became detached from his spinal cord, and he spent two months in a coma. He emerged as a quadriplegic boy struggling to regain capacities for life on earth. He became the youngest person to have an operation that let him breathe on his own, without a ventilator, and continued recovering to the point that he was able to stand upright and even walk on a treadmill. His story is a testimony to progress in medical science and the resilience of the human spirit. But this was not the story they decided to publish.

Instead, with encouragement from a literary agent, father and son wrote about Alex's journey into the afterlife. The book included some captivating details, such as the shape of the angels' wings, the skyline of the heavenly city, and the devil's moldy teeth. A TV movie was made, and a million copies were sold of the book, *The Boy Who Came Back from Heaven: A True Story*. True, however, is one thing the story was not.

At first, the boy himself tried to warn people. A year after the book's publication, he wrote to its fans on Facebook, "1 of the most deceptive books ever." His comment was deleted, and his name was blocked from the Facebook page. Four years later, Alex recanted more fully: "I did not die. I did not go to heaven. I said I went to heaven because I thought it would get me attention. When I made the claims that I did, I had never read the Bible. People have profited from lies, and continue to. They should read the Bible, which is enough."[6] At this point, Tyndale House stopped selling the book.

Perhaps more doubt and investigation up front might have prevented deeper disappointment down the road. The conclusion is not that faith must always constrict itself to the rules of science or that science is the only path to knowledge. Reality exceeds what science can grasp. However, a scientific sensibility can help to curb the credulity and exaggerating tendency of faith.

Malarkeys aside, a number of other people claim to have had near-death experiences during which they beheld amazing things, including glimpses of an afterlife. How do scientists approach these phenomena? Let's say a person emerges from a coma or even undergoes cardiac death and is then revived. These events do not happen every day, but they do happen frequently enough to be studied and classified. Some people report leaving their physical body. Some recount floating upward and looking down on their lifeless body lying on the operating table. Some speak of entering tunnels and seeing brilliant light. Communication with loved ones who have died is another common feature of these near-death experiences. Perhaps most odd, some people report knowledge of conversations between medical staff in the hospital or of other events taking

---

[6] "'The Boy Who Came Back from Heaven' Recants Story, Rebukes Christian Retailers," *Pulpit and Pen*, January 13, 2015, https://tinyurl.com/oecg5gf.

place in the world outside—knowledge that no person lying in a coma should be able to possess, physically speaking.

An experience like this can lift the fear of death and turn skeptics into believers. But the scientific mind is inclined to probe further, whether driven by disbelief in the spiritual realm or belief that the physical realm holds untold complexity and mystery. In either case, proceeding along physical lines, here is one way scientists might investigate near-death experiences.

First, let's construct a tray and place assorted trinkets on it, such as little colored balls or playing cards. Then suspend the tray from the ceiling of the operating room, so that its contents are not visible from the ground up, but only from the ceiling looking down. Next, wait until some patient reports having an out-of-body experience during an operation or while in a coma. If the patient says, "I was floating above the room," we will ask the patient to identify the contents of the tray. Accurate identification would yield objective evidence. This kind of research is currently taking place.

Some people will say this approach is going too far. We cannot expect science to prove everything that faith affirms. This point is well taken, but by the same token, we should not rush to tell youth that science *has* proven this or that aspect of faith without first consulting actual scientists. Even when skeptical, scientists are often willing to investigate. If there is funding, there will be research. One thing that propels research into near-death experiences is the fact that scientists have discovered cases where the heart stops beating for some minutes and cortical activity of the brain becomes isoelectric (in other words, the patient is in a very deep coma) yet this patient is somehow able to know things that were happening in the outside world.

Many scientists have supposed the "spiritual" elements of near-death experiences were actually hallucinations caused by the brain being damaged, or the brain overheating, or perhaps drugs injected into the patient. But the hallucination hypothesis has holes. At least some patients whose brains should have no awareness of the outside words are in fact able to recall external events that are real and verifiable. Further, as medical researcher Sam Parnia notes, two studies based on an examination of memory quality "both concluded that NDE [near-death experience] recollections are not consistent with illusory experiences but with memories of real life events."[7]

In general and in conclusion, the scientific sensibility is careful and measured, slow to draw conclusions and quick to point out the need for further research. This sensibility can help us to be sober minded about the claims we make in church.

Yet for all its value, science is not enough. Youth need the knowledge that comes by way of faith—today more than ever. The reason why is the next topic.

[7] Sam Parnia, "Understanding the Cognitive Experience of Death and the Near-Death Experience" *QJM: An International Journal of Medicine*, Volume 110, Issue 2, Feb. 2017, 67–69.

CHAPTER 3

What Science Cannot Do

We expect so much from science. In focus groups, teenagers were asked, How would you respond if an asteroid were about to hit the earth, bringing a certain end to human life? What would you do? Get right with God? Draw close to people you love? Make a few final posts to your social media accounts? Many youth responded simply by doubting the scenario. Surely, they said, scientists would be able to figure out a way to stop this crisis from happening.

Yet all our knowledge of the natural world has not prevented ecologic crisis. Our knowing how to produce more material goods has not prevented the economic crisis of vast disparity between wealthy and poor in the world. Science and technology have not taught us how to love one another or how to speak tenderly to one another. Science and technology have not given us an overarching telos or purpose to life.

Friedrich Nietzsche, though hardly known for his optimism, once remarked, "The person who has a why to live for can bear almost any how." This "why" seems too often missing today. Thanks to modern science and technology, youth know the answers to more *how* questions than any generation in history. But modern science and technology were never designed to produce an entire worldview or to tell us of reality in its totality. They were never designed to tell us why we live. Perhaps we have tried to make science more than it could be and so made ourselves less than we should be.

It is high time, therefore, to teach young people about the deep things of God. Why? Because they already sense a reality that is not physical. Because they long for intimacy. And because all of us want to go higher and deeper than the physical eye can see. In an age of science, still the Spirit of God calls to us, deep to deep.

When we examine a typical identity crisis of adolescence or the various crises of wider society, it becomes clear that science and technology alone cannot save us. Youth are searching for purpose and also for power—not just technological power but spiritual power to enact budding and blossoming feelings of devotion and compassion. They are searching for meaning in life that extends beyond what science and technology can supply.

While faith may be apt to inflate and exaggerate, modern science tends to simplify and reduce. Just as science can help correct the exaggerating tendency of faith, so faith is needed to correct the reducing tendency of science. Scientists in the physical sciences (such as physics, chemistry, and biology) use physical instruments and their physical senses to probe physical phenomena. In reducing their scope to what is physical, they intentionally screen out the realm of the spiritual.[1] This is why an age of science and technology needs the knowledge of God, now more than ever—not to fill unexplained gaps in the physical universe but to fill a gaping hole in human existence. God works in and through the physical realm but in ways seen only through eyes of the heart.

Einstein reportedly remarked, "Everything should be made as simple as possible, but not simpler." In general, scientists reduce reality to its physical dimensions and then try to explain as much as possible as simply as possible. A case in point is Einstein's famous $E = mc^2$. The energy of an atom equals its mass times the speed of light squared. This simple

---

[1] This statement is most true of scientists working in the physical or "hard" sciences, such as physics, chemistry, and biology. The social sciences, such as psychology or sociology, still speak of invisible ideas, feelings, and emotions. Even here we see prejudice in favor of the physical—hence the pull of psychology toward neuroscience.

equation contains mind-blowing, and potentially world-destroying, ramifications. It is the theory behind the atomic bomb.

"But not simpler"—the second half of Einstein's statement warns against oversimplifying. Simplifying brings clarity, but oversimplifying causes distortion. Reduce too much and something vital gets lost. Stephen Hawking may have had Einstein's aphorism in the back of his mind when he predicted, in the year 2000, that the "next century will be the century of complexity." DNA molecules, for instance, are very small but massively complex. Yet even in dealing with complex things, scientists strive for maximum clarity and simplicity.

Here is another way of putting it: scientists like to use "Occam's razor" to shave off excess. Occam refers to William of Occam, a fourteenth-century Franciscan friar and philosopher who proposed that the simplest solution to a problem is usually the right one. Right or wrong, simpler hypotheses are preferred because they are easier to test. Modern science greatly reduces the types of questions it asks—and answers it offers—in order to arrive at questions and answers that are testable.

We are so used to thinking of science this way, as grounded in observation and experimentation, that it is hard to imagine any other way. But until the modern period, there was another way, and the person who exemplified it best was someone who was born before Jesus, yet he exerted an enormous influence on both the church and the development of science. His name was Aristotle.

Aristotle spoke of four factors (*aitia*) or causes that make a thing what it is: matter, motion, design, and purpose. A house, for example, is caused by physical matter such as wood and nails, and it is caused by physical motion such as sawing and hammering. But equally a house is caused by its design or blueprint, and furthermore, it is caused by its ultimate purpose. Why, after all, does a house really exist? To become a home for people. Being a home is the final, or telic, cause of a house. For Aristotle and his followers, this "purpose" cause is not just something in the mind. It is an actual ordering force in the universe.

Science today does not study reality this way. Modern science directs its attention to questions of matter and motion, not questions of ultimate meaning or purpose. After all, I might say the purpose of a house is to provide a home, but the house builder may say it is to provide an income. At least we can agree that a house needs hammers and nails to exist. Modern science stays mute on issues of ultimate purpose. In contrast to ancient science, modern science asks questions that can be answered by empirical methods of observation, manipulation, testing, and measurement. Physics uses time but does not probe the ultimate meaning of time. Biology studies life but not the ultimate purpose of life. This is a dramatic shift.

To put the dramatic shift as simply as possible: in modern science, all *why* questions automatically get turned into *how* questions. Why does an apple fall to the ground instead of flying upward? Because of how gravity operates on earth. Why are people living on earth? Because of how genes operate over time. This shift has a profound effect on science—and on modern thinking. Reducing why questions to how questions changes our sense of what is really real. Matter and motion are objective facts of life, whereas the grand design and ultimate meaning of life are felt to be subjective opinions.

By contrast, in the days of Aristotle and up to the modern period, every bit of matter or flit of motion was presumed to have purpose. Physical objects had metaphysical destinies. A thing was not just pushed by its physical causes. It was pulled and drawn toward some fulfillment by its final, telic cause. In keeping with Aristotle, people sensed that earthy things were pulled downward to the earth, where they belong, whereas airy things were pulled upward. Rocks and falling apples were drawn toward the earth, their natural resting place. People were drawn toward God. As Augustine had said, "Our hearts are restless till they find their rest in Thee."

In this earlier science, people used concepts such as goodness and justice to describe the order of the universe. In the modern era, these metaphysical considerations get stripped away in favor of better physical explanations. Gravity explains how and why apples fall to the ground. Apples don't need a better reason. The goodness of apples, justice of apples, and ultimate purpose of apples are not concerns for modern science. With apples, this approach seems to work fairly well. But does it work as well with people?

When Stephen Hawking died in 2018, his children, Lucy, Robert, and Tim, issued a statement: "We are deeply saddened that our beloved father passed away today." Praising their father's intelligence and goodness of character, they recalled, "He once said, 'It would not be much of a universe if it wasn't home to the people you love.' We will miss him forever."[2]

Where does this unscientific-sounding language come from? *Beloved . . . deeply . . . passed away . . . home . . . forever.* This language arises from a Christian sense of reality. Hawking was an atheist, but these words comport with the Christian history of England, where he and his children grew up. At the hour of death, $E = mc^2$ does not adequately sum up the energy of a human lifetime. At the hour of death, we summon this other sense of reality. And in reality, given a 13.8 billion–year scheme of the universe, we are very close, at this very moment, to the hour of death.

In conclusion, science cannot tell us that the universe is a home or that a father will be missed forever. These are not testable hypotheses but assertions of faith. Faith consistently recoils against the reducing tendency of science.

The aim here is not to denigrate the methods of science but to tell young people why an age of science needs faith now more than ever. When modern science pruned away spiritual and metaphysical concerns to focus on the physical universe, it became remarkably more accurate and efficient. We now have much more knowledge of the physical universe and, through technology, a stupendous ability to alter our environment and improve economic standards of living. This is a large benefit from which there is no turning back. But the large benefit conceals an equally large deficit.

The deficit becomes apparent if we imagine a world where people know more and more about how things operate but less and less about why

---

[2] Andrew Griffin and Chris Stevenson, "Stephen Hawking: Physicist Heralded as One of the Greatest Scientific Minds Ever Dies Aged 76," *The Independent,* March 14, 2018, https://tinyurl.com/y93k9alo.

anything matters. Or a world in which people have mastered instruments of technology but feel hopelessly adrift when it comes to concepts of goodness, justice, and love. If a building is burning or a trolley car is hurtling out of control, and you must choose between saving a person or a pet, which would it be? In repeated psychological tests, people struggle mightily with these scenarios. In one test by research psychologist Richard Toploski, 40 percent of adults said they would save a pet with which they had an emotional bond over a person who was a foreign tourist.[3]

These are just fantasy situations, but they shed light on moral thinking. Joan Dunayer, who opposes speciesism, says the only good option in this horrible scenario would be to reach quickly into your pocket and flip a coin. Humans and animals, she contends, have the same moral value.[4] Even if a group of church youth decide she is wrong, they may struggle to agree why. The youth may just say their feelings are different from Dunayer's. It all seems so confusing. Because science stays mute on most moral questions, these questions feel unanswerable.

Along with moral issues, questions of meaning are similarly confounding. What is the meaning or purpose of my life? This is a pressing question in adolescence, and if no answer is forthcoming, it can be a fairly short step from thinking my life is meaningless to feeling it is hopeless. The opportunity and even urgency of ministry is this: to help youth see how there is more to God's reality than meets the eye—more meaning and purpose, more power and love, more goodness and love (and also more evil) than our modern scientific methods can detect. Science intentionally reduces its questions to the physical realm, thus to uncover its hidden wonders. But people of faith are called upon to uncover and disclose for young people the deep things of God. Just as science can correct the exaggerating tendency of believers, so faith can correct the reducing tendency of a scientific mindset.

[3] Hal Herzog, "Would You Save a Puppy or Child from a Burning Building? A New Study Shows When We Choose Pets over People," *Psychology Today*, June 17, 2013, https://tinyurl.com/yd28uy64.
[4] Herzog, "Would You Save a Puppy or Child?"

To be clear and at risk of repetition: the reducing tendency of science, in and of itself, serves an excellent purpose. Just as the microscope and telescope are cylinders that limit the scope of vision in order to amplify vision, so too natural science as a whole limits its questions in order to isolate and analyze what falls within its range. It seems reality is constructed in such a way that even finite things (such as molecules) are incredibly ordered, complex, and somehow unlimited, and the human mind is constructed in such a way that scientists can gladly appreciate this fact.

The problem is not the reduced range of modern science but rather a tendency to reduce all of reality to what science can see. The problem is not the restricted inquiry of science but the overreaching authority of some scientists, whose brilliance and expertise are thought to extend into every corner of life and death. As a case in point, the next chapter describes the tragicomedy that unfolds when Richard Dawkins is teaching youth about biological evolution and the discussion turns toward the meaning of life.

CHAPTER 4

The Meaning of Life

E nter, via YouTube, a London classroom where Professor Dawkins is saying "good morning" to a group of teenagers of Anglo-Saxon and East Asian ethnicities. As the camera bobs around the room, girls and boys in blue blazers stay seated and still, respectful eyes focused forward, attentive ears listening as the good professor rehearses some basic facts about the universe. It is, he says, about fourteen billion years old. It has, he notes, innumerable stars and planets. But perhaps only one planet, ours, has this strange thing called life. (Microbial life on exoplanets is not mentioned.) He asks, "What is different about this planet?" Then he supplies the answer: "Nobody knew until about the middle of the nineteenth century, when Charles Darwin finally worked it out. . . . Ever since then we've gradually been filling in the details, and now it is absolutely certain that Darwin was right. And now we essentially understand why we are all here, what life is all about, what is the meaning of it all."[1]

Dawkins's first assertion—that evolution tells us "why we are all here"—makes perfect sense once we recall that he is a modern scientist who turns why questions into how questions. But why on earth does he

---

[1] "Richard Dawkins Teaching Evolution to Religious Students," YouTube video, posted November 16, 2014, https://tinyurl.com/q629fue.

also claim that evolution tells us "what life is all about" and "the meaning of it all" when clearly evolution has no stake in these issues?

A simple explanation would be that Dawkins misspoke. Even polished public speakers may grow nervous in front of teenagers. Or perhaps his ardent advocacy for neo-Darwinian evolution has caused him to exaggerate by claiming more for Darwin's theory than Darwin did. At any rate, he gets another crack at the question a few minutes later when one girl politely raises her hand to ask, "How does evolution fit into the meaning of life? What is the meaning of life if your—"

"What is the meaning of life on an evolutionary worldview?" Dawkins repeats, seizing her question in midsentence. The question seems to animate him, for he replies at length, "One thing to say is that the universe doesn't owe us any meaning. It could be that there is no meaning of life. And if so, that would be just tough." He pauses, offers a sympathetic smile, and then continues:

I don't think that, because I think that we can all make whatever meaning we choose to make. And you, each of you, will have plenty of meanings in your own life. You'll be enthusiastic about some things. Maybe some sport you play. Maybe some books you read. Maybe your love life. Maybe your family life. Maybe some of you love nature; some of you love music. These are all individual meanings that you can give to your life. That doesn't mean that life itself has one special meaning. It doesn't mean that we are here for any particular purpose, any more than mountains are here for a purpose or rocks are here for a purpose. Rocks are just here. . . .

There is a sense in which life is just here. Life came about through the evolutionary process, but after billions of years of evolution, life-forms arose that have big brains, big nervous systems, and we've got the biggest brains of all for our size, and so our brains are capable of developing purposes of our own. We with our big brains can think of our own purposes. We can aim at things in life. We can have a grand design for the whole of our life, which is the privilege that we enjoy because our brains are so big. And the reason our brains are so big is that evolution gave us big brains. Over a very, very long period of time, the brains of our ancestors got gradually bigger and bigger and bigger, until they became so big that they are now capable of enjoying music and poetry and mathematics and love and all the things that give our lives meaning and give our lives our own individual purpose.

The camera does not pan back to the girl to catch her reaction. We cannot tell whether she is smiling or frowning at his reply to her question.

On the one hand, she may be very happy with the answer she has just heard. When it comes to the meaning of life, you as a teenager get to decide for yourself, and who doesn't like a free choice? You can follow your particular passions or individual interests. Whatever you enjoy, whomever you love, can become the individual meaning of your individual life. The girl could be smiling. On the other hand, she could be thinking, and the more she is thinking, the more likely she is to be frowning.

If I can point to anything at all out there—whether sports, books, family, music, nature, or another person—and call it the meaning of my life, then clearly the meaning of my life is not really out there at all. It is something I fabricate with my brain. Dawkins says as much. He does not merely describe scientifically how the brain enables us to ponder life's meaning. Rather, he asserts that the human brain is itself the source and creator, the Alpha and Omega, of the meaning of life. The cosmos may be incredibly vast, but its entire meaning can be contained within an organ the size of a shoebox, shape of a walnut, and consistency of room temperature butter.[2]

What does it all mean? As an individual, you get to decide with your big brain and nervous system, which may sound great, but don't forget this one fact: any meaning that exists in your brain, as a result of your brain, will cease to exist or be meaningful as soon as your brain dies, which is very soon. Even if the human brain took billions of years to come to

[2] Barbara Bruce, *Our Spiritual Brain: Integrating Brain Research and Faith Development* (Nashville: Abingdon, 2002), 21.

life, it still takes less than a hundred to turn to mush. So what meaning is there, really and truly? We have a word for something that exists only in the brain, a word that Dawkins himself helped to popularize. It is called a delusion.

Now some philosophers would argue strenuously that a humanly fabricated (as opposed to God-given) meaning of life can be authentic and not a delusion at all. They would argue that meaning is no less valid or valuable if it exists only in the mind by an individual's existential choice. Their arguments may be strong enough to keep you from killing yourself. Paradoxically, however, the premier proponents of this atheistic existential school have also argued that suicide is, in fact, the most authentic and meaningful action you can take in response to a universe that declares your life to be pointless and absurd. The universe makes this declaration by its brute silence. Pascal, as we recall, is terrified not by the infinite space of the universe but by its silence.

It would take a very different reading of reality to hear the universe declaring God's praises (Ps 19:1). A very different reading of reality is needed to see God gesturing with open arms to the impossibly vast cosmos and declaring to humankind, "This is how much I love you!"

Modern science does not refute this latter reading but simply ignores it. Talk of God falls outside its range. Fair enough—but a reduction of reality occurs when the simplifying, limiting tendency of science is combined with other ideas and assumptions. If people assume that only science gives us public truth, then it is easy to suppose that convictions about God-given meaning and purpose are just private opinions. If people assume that scientists are the smartest and best public intellectuals, then we might suppose they are qualified to make pronouncements about big metaphysical questions such as, well, the meaning of life.

Here we intend no disrespect to either Dr. Dawkins or his very large brain. His books once sold millions of copies, in part because he gave voice to anti-religious ideas that many people were thinking but afraid to say. His brain, like yours and mine, contains billions of neurons and is capable of amazing feats. The brain is a marvelous instrument, just as the telescope is, in its way, as marvelous as the stars it observes. But the instrument is the means, not the end. We build telescopes in order to see the stars. We have brains in order to perceive God and the amplitude of God's creation.

Without being anti-scientific, we can help youth trust some of their spiritual intuitions. We notice, for instance, how the girl in the London classroom posed her question. She asked, "What is *the* meaning of life?" Her question is traditionally a religious one. It presupposes that life as a whole, for all people, has some singular meaning. She is asking about one overarching telos of human existence. He responds by pointing to sundry loci of human enjoyment. She is asking for meaning beyond herself. He responds by pointing to her brain and nervous system. Her question and his answer are coming from two different universes, two different thought worlds. Yes, books, sports, family, nature, friends are all meaningful and important—but why? Really, why? Even if a young person has not found the answer, the ability to ask this question shows that the eyes of the heart are not completely in the dark.

Like Paul in Ephesians, we can pray for more light. And we can also offer instruction. We have a beautiful, God-given opportunity to show how faith and science can illuminate and correct each other. Still, as with any door of effective ministry, there are large obstacles (1 Cor 16:9). Facing them squarely is the next topic.

CHAPTER 5

Science against Faith

A re science and religion "often in conflict"? Pew Research found that 59 percent of Americans said yes to this question.[1] The sense of conflict rises slightly among eighteen- to twenty-three-year-olds, according to the National Study of Youth and Religion.

The research contained a few surprises. Overall, conservative Protestants are as pro-science as anyone else.[2] Conservative or liberal, devout believers are actually less likely to see conflict than those with no religious affiliation. Devout or not, most people see conflict between faith and science as something that goes on around them, not something that causes them personal distress. A typical response would be "I know other people think religion and science are in conflict, but I myself don't have that problem."

However, in these next pages, I want to propose that the relationship between faith and science does present a personal problem for young people today, even if they feel no conscious turmoil and even if they see no obvious conflict.

---

[1] "Perception of Conflict between Science and Religion," Pew Research Center, Religion and Science, October 22, 2015, https://tinyurl.com/ybpofxqb.
[2] Jonathan Hill, *Emerging Adulthood and Faith* (Grand Rapids, MI: Calvin College Press, 2015), 50.

We can start by noting some similarities and differences between religion and science. Both search for truth. Both summon passion and personal commitment. Both delight in discovery. Both may begin and end in wonder. These are just a few salient similarities.

At the same time, we note significant differences. In science, we are becoming more conscious of the universe; in faith, more conscious of God. Science may point a few people toward God, and faith can enhance our awareness of the universe, but on the whole science and faith have different objects of desire. More important, they have different rules for what counts as persuasive evidence. Science makes arguments based on empirical methods of observation and testing, whereas faith often rests its case on revelations contained in sacred texts and traditions.

This last distinction may be a bit too simple. Science is also rooted in its tradition. As Michael Polanyi has shown, scientists participate in a scientific community where habits of mind are passed down, one generation to the next. And faith, for its part, has its own kind of empirical testing. Believers are told not to believe everything but to test everything (1 Thess 5:21). Still, as a general rule, we can say science starts with a physical universe and proceeds by way of observation, whereas faith starts with a spiritual universe, proceeds by way of reason and revelation, and so comes to include "conviction of things not seen" (Heb 11:1).

Because they have different objects of desire and different rules of evidence, science and faith see things differently, even when looking at the same thing. In science, energy is a quantity producing light or heat. In theology, energy is a quality producing good or evil. Does it even make sense to use the same word in both contexts?

Furthermore, neither faith nor science is monolithic. Faith (*pistis*) carries a range of meanings in the New Testament. Faith is the knowledge of things not seen—but also the power to move mountains. Faith is the total fidelity (or faithfulness) of Jesus in accepting crucifixion—and also the total commitment of believers in accepting Jesus. In this book, "faith" is shorthand for the reality that Christians see through the eyes of their heart.

The word *science* also carries a range of meanings. After all, what is science essentially? Each philosopher of science seems to give us some aspect of the elephant—refutable conjectures (Karl Popper), progressive research programs (Imre Lakatos), empirical adequacy (Bas van Fraassen), pragmatic success (Richard Rorty)—but not the whole.[3] People may carry the everyday notion that science means simply looking at evidence you can see, but on closer inspection, this idea of observable evidence gets fuzzier. Seeing repeated tests in a laboratory is different from observing the historical evidence of fossils, or the evidence of gene maps, or the simulations produced by computer models, or the ongoing activity of subjects in the field. Yet all these observations and computations, with their differing degrees of mathematical precision and subjective judgment, are said to be scientific.

Not everything believed in science can be seen, and not everything can be put into formulas. We have a general sense that science entails a virtuous cycle involving observations, hypotheses, predictions, and evidence. But the meaning of science becomes more elusive when one tries to pin down the particulars.

Some scientists will say that science is simply what scientists do, which sounds inane but actually gets at some vital features. Back to Polanyi's point: science is done by people within a community who carry on an evolving tradition that gets passed down, one generation to the next. Most scientists are not philosophers of science. They care more about things in nature than the nature of science. In this book, "science" is shorthand for the reality that scientists see through their physical senses.

In sum, science and faith both have traditions, and at one time in Christian history, they shared the same tradition; however, in recent centuries, they have taken divergent roads toward knowing reality. Scientists do not weigh the Scriptures and lived experience of the church any more than Christians try to analyze God's love in a test tube. Modern science has a tradition of asking how, not why. It has a tradition of doubting and skepticism, of favoring "objective" evidence over personal testimony, and of striving for measurable results. Modern science lives exclusively in

---

[3] John Polkinghorne, *Belief in God in an Age of Science* (New Haven, CT: Yale University Press, 1998), 104–5.

the physical universe. Faith dwells in a spiritual universe, where the evidence certainly does include personal testimony as well as many immeasurable elements, such as love, joy, peace, patience, goodness, etc.—the manifold fruit of the Holy Spirit.

Thus the overall difference between faith and science is stark—seeing physically versus seeing spiritually—yet this difference alone does not explain conflicts that arise. Rather, the fervency that scientists and believers hold in common may be the greater hindrance to seeing each other's perspectives. Both faith and science summon intensity, passion, and tenacity. These same qualities sustain both scientists and believers through seasons of enormous frustration. But a singular, passionate focus can make some scientists and some believers act like teenagers in love—willing to scale any mountain but unwilling to brook any counterargument or alternate way to see reality.

We can help scientists and faithful people to hear each other, and help young people to see both perspectives, if we keep in mind that faith and science have different goals and different rules for how to arrive at truth. Further, it will help tremendously if we can see and explain to youth how each outlook tends to occlude or screen out the other.

Take scientists first. Whenever their knowledge hits a wall, scientists try to climb it. They are committed to relentless interrogation until the universe yields its secrets. The path they travel is physical, and they are rigorous in sticking to it. Any appeal to God in order to account for some gap in their knowledge strikes scientists as lazy thinking. They are trying to say how things happen. To say "God did it" solves nothing but only raises the obvious question of *how* God did it, which makes the problem of explanation harder, not simpler, because now you have to explain God as well as the thing at hand. We will wait in vain for scientists to point to anything they cannot explain and then exclaim, "Here God is acting!"

Scientists in fields such as physics, chemistry, and biology are all materialists—not in the sense that they all drive Mercedes but because they focus exclusively on the material world of matter and motion. They may not be strict materialists in their love life or church life, but they most definitely are in their laboratories. This passion for finding physical explanations via scientific methods can cause them to cultivate mental habits that obstruct religious faith. Following are three such habits and corresponding obstacles to faith.

First, the scientific mind may be inclined to treat God as a hypothesis. In this case, God's existence, like some force within the physical universe, would need to be proven, just like other scientific hypotheses. However, for the vast majority of Christians, and in the bulk of Christian tradition, God is not a hypothesis to be proven but a Person to be met. For most Christian discourse, God is the premise or starting place, not the conclusion. Of course, every starting place can be doubted. If we start with God, we can doubt that God is real. If we start with human reason, we can doubt the worth of rationality.

Perhaps due to doubts, there is a subset of Christian theology, called natural theology, that has tried to prove God's existence and the reasonableness of faith by using both deductive reason and inductive investigations of nature. These arguments, like Pascal's famous wager,[4] may work better at reassuring believers than convincing nonbelievers. Believers are people who have already met God, at least once. Science might try to view God as a hypothesis, but for Christian believers, God is a Person (in the language of theology, a *hypostasis*). This difference in outlooks sets the stage for potential conflict.

As a second obstacle, the scientific mind may be inclined to treat religion as a primitive form of science. This notion gets heavily promoted by some popular science writers with an atheist agenda. Religion, they will say, was an early, superstitious attempt to explain nature and to control

[4] Here is Pascal's argument, in simple form. You have to bet your life on whether God exists. Option one: you bet that God *does* exist. If it turns out you are right, you stand to receive an infinite gain (eternity in heaven). If it turns out you are wrong, you will have suffered only a finite loss (a few forsaken earthly indulgences). Option two: you bet that God does *not* exist. If it turns out you are right, you may have gotten a finite gain (earthly indulgences)—but if you are wrong, you stand to suffer an infinite loss (eternity in hell). Therefore, option one is the rational choice.

Pascal did not actually intend this argument to persuade anyone to believe in God. He was simply trying to refute people who claimed belief in God is irrational. He was saying, "Okay, if you want to be rational about it, consider this: your whole life is one big wager. What if you bet against God's existence and lose?" But Pascal did not see his own faith as a bet. He came to faith by direct reasoning of the heart. Other kinds of reasoning, like the wager argument, were simply helpful in quieting internal doubts and external doubters.

forces in nature. Then science came along to provide the right explanations, and technology came along to offer the better means of control. *Le voilà*—people are now free to mature intellectually and outgrow religion.

Yet this account rings false with regard to Christian faith. Anyone who has actually read the Bible can attest that explaining nature is not very high on the agenda. The goal of most Christian writings is not to explain nature but more to narrate what feels inexplicable. Jesus comes to people, and suddenly or gradually, they experience joy in the midst of sorrow, hope in the place of despair, forgiveness in the face of horrendous wrongdoing. The aim of Christian teaching is not to explain the mechanics of how these events happen—God's grace is usually a sufficient reason—but rather to help people live more fully into this new reality.

To be sure, religious people have traditionally made connections between God's activity and certain events in nature (called "acts of God"). Since more events in nature now have physical explanations, it may feel as if science is squeezing God out of the picture. But this problem is largely a modern fabrication, in that it comes from trying to draw boundary lines between natural "God-free" events and supernatural "God-caused" events. There is an ancient mindset, still available to us today, that perceives God acting in and through the everyday realm of nature.

In biblical times, miracles were seen as God's extraordinary actions, but everyday life displayed God's ordinary activity. Jesus says God makes the sun to shine on the evil and the good. God sends the rain upon the just and unjust (Matt 5:45). A better scientific understanding of weather systems or solar systems does not nullify Christ's words, for he is describing God's purposeful activity within the natural sphere. Even quotidian, scientifically describable events in nature can carry a surplus of feeling and meaning—the beauty or wonder or horror of it all—which leads even nonbelievers like Dawkins to call themselves "deeply religious" in this poetic sense.

We need to be careful here. I would not want to reduce theology to poetics or aesthetics, as if to imply God were not really acting. God could be exerting force at some unseen quantum or macro level, but the point is this: the eyes of the heart want to see why more than how. When it comes to divine action, faith cares less about the mechanics than the pattern and purpose. The mechanics inevitably pull us down to the level of matter and motion, whereas the pattern and purpose draw us upward to the love, joy, and peace of Christ, which exceed mechanical know-how. In short, it is a mistake to think of theology as a primitive form of science, and this mistake can provoke unnecessary conflict between faith and science.

As a third obstacle, the scientific mind may be inclined to slide from science into scientism. Science refers to proven methods for knowing physical reality. Scientism, on the other hand, is an exaggerated faith in science and/or the belief that all reality is circumscribed by what science can see. We can chart the hubris that leads from science to scientism. Science, which begins as a good way to know many things, becomes the best way to know all things and then the only way to know anything—because, it is decided, whatever things science cannot study also cannot possibly exist. To use philosophical terms: the scientific epistemology yields an ontology and axiology in which only matter really matters, and the immaterial realm becomes immaterial.

The notion that only science can yield knowledge is flawed. It is unproven, scientifically or otherwise. Certainly science has expanded our knowledge exponentially, but what if there are vast continents of reality unreachable by scientific vessels? What if life holds radiant possibilities only faith can apprehend? These are valid questions, but scientism would have us believe that science is our only snorkel to reality. Not just some professional scientists but also many members of the wider public hold this view. By adopting the exaggerating tendency of true believers, these believers in the powers of science suppose that only scientific knowledge is valid.

Nothing fuels this tumid trust in science more than technology. All the computing power used to send men to the moon can now fit neatly into a teenager's pants pocket. Scientism points to miracles of technology as reason to have confidence not only in science but solely in science. Today, as always, life is full of problems, but today more than ever, people are inclined to think problems can be solved by science and technology. Is there any problem, individual or global, where a technological solution is not being worked on? Whatever the problem, within or without, there must be some device we can make or pill we can take. Even when technological progress has been the source of problems, we look for further technological progress to solve them. Even the universal and intractable problem of human mortality is not beyond the purview of technology. Some "transhumanists" offer confident predictions that soon and very soon, humans will be able to overcome physical death by uploading our brain matter onto synthetic neurons housed in robotic bodies. Our hope is built on nothing less than computer code and silicon chips (or some supermaterial superior to silicon).

But it is easy to spot cracks in the belief structure of scientism. Fifteen or twenty years ago, one could read eupeptic predictions that the technologies of cell phones and social media were shaping youth into the friendliest, best-informed generation in history. Then newer reports came in indicating that cell phones, social media, and other digital technologies were contributing to unprecedented levels of adolescent anxiety, depression, and suicide. Because technology changes so rapidly, it is hard to gauge its effect on rising generations. Good studies take time, and they require good follow-up studies, which take more time. Meanwhile, newer technologies are arriving on the scene to shape young minds in still newer ways. By the time this book is out, further data will likely be telling parents and pastors something new about teens and technology—either very good or very bad, since those stories sell the best.

At any rate, it can feel as if we are living in an age of both technological nirvana and all-consuming technological crisis. In another century, people may have viewed developments with unbridled optimism. Science led to technology, and technology always spelled progress. But today it is clear the climate has been changing. Science has also led to scientism and to an exaggerated trust in scientific and technological progress and in turn to a backlash of disappointment and mistrust. When science fiction and fantasy series for young people portray some future technological era, it is predictably a dystopic, hellish city painted in tones that are bleak and gray, depicting forces that are metallic and dehumanizing. In the midst of this dystopia, one or two heroic youth arise to rebel against the technocracy, carried aloft by intuitions of a spiritual universe, a realm of meaning and purpose, where sacrifice, loyalty, and love still prevail.

Admittedly, cinematic love is usually romantic, not Christian, but still it tells us something important about the ingrained youthful impulse to transcend a physical world reduced to matter and motion. Young people are drawn toward books and films where the heroes are hopeful, courageous, and strong enough to stand against mechanistic forces. Without disparaging the accomplishments of science and technology with respect to the physical universe, we can invite youth more fully into the spiritual universe they long to see, which is to say more fully into the presence of God.

In sum, the scientific mind is inclined to treat God as a hypothesis, to treat religion as primitive science, and to slide from science into scientism. None of these problems pertains to all scientists, but they are tendencies of a scientific age that can affect any and all youth—not youth alone but perhaps youth more acutely. For developmental reasons, adolescence is a time of questioning authority. Science has a long tradition of questioning authority, while religion, especially in its ethical dimensions, is an authority figure. When some scientists portray religion as a primitive form of science and science as the rightful replacement to religion, this misconstrual can engender or intensify a sense of conflict among adolescents. Ministry with youth means helping them recognize and understand these three distortions coming from the side of science.

At the same time, we must admit that distortion can run the other way as well. Just as scientifically minded people can misunderstand and misrepresent faith, so too some Christian teachers can give young people wrong impressions of science. This problem is the next topic.

CHAPTER 6

Faith against Science

When I was in eighth grade, our English class read *Inherit the Wind*, a play about the famous *Scopes* trial that took place in Tennessee in 1925. This trial became the flashpoint of national controversy over teaching evolution in public schools, and it commenced a cultural history that is still embedded in present-day antagonisms between progressive and conservative Christians.

As an aspiring journalist, I paid particular attention to one of the play's characters, a reporter named E. K. Hornbeck, who was a fictionalized version of H. L. Mencken, the eminent real-life journalist who depicted the cultural landscape of early twentieth-century America. My father, also a journalist, had taught me that good reporters should strive to be objective and not insert their personal opinions. But this Hornbeck character had more in common with newsfeeds of today, where an "analysis" of the news supersedes actual reporting. Hornbeck made no effort to hide his disdain for the biblical beliefs of the rural folk in Dayton, Tennessee. I recall his views were echoed by my English teacher in Princeton, New Jersey.

As a shy Christian convert, I felt quietly bothered. I didn't fully buy the narrative of scientific progress triumphing over religious dogma, and I hoped the real-life H. L. Mencken might be friendlier toward believers like me. I had hoped wrong. The real-life Mencken, as I later learned, had no less scorn for the town of Dayton ("a ninth-rate country town") and the fundamental Christians who lived there. He wrote, "Faith cannot only move mountains; it can also soothe the distressed spirits of mountaineers." From this clever turn of phrase, Mencken goes on to describe their faith: "They believe that they are not mammals. They believe, on Bryan's word [William Jennings Bryan was a lawyer in the *Scopes* trial], that they know more than all the men of science of Christendom. They believe, on the authority of Genesis, that the earth is flat and that witches still infest it. They believe, finally and especially, that all who doubt these great facts of revelation will go to hell. So they are consoled."[1]

These words are part of a protracted culture war between liberal and conservative Christianity in America that continues to this day. While deriding fundamental Christians, Mencken shines praise on liberal, progressive "educated clergy: Episcopalians, Unitarians, Jews, and so on."

The *Scopes* trial thus demonstrates an important feature of American culture. Conflicts between faith and science are often primarily conflicts between faith and faith—between different views of the Bible and of what it means to call yourself a Christian. Regarding the *Scopes* trial, certain ironies tend to subvert a simplistic narrative in which the enlightenment of science overcomes the intransigence of old-time, young-earth religion.

For one thing, the State of Tennessee had assigned the textbook that included the unlawful chapter on evolution. For his part, John T. Scopes said after the trial that he had in fact skipped over that chapter in the classroom. But the American Civil Liberties Union had wanted a test case, and Scopes was willing. Most poignantly, the textbook itself, entitled *Civic Biology*, was blatantly racist. Veering from biology into social policy, it asserted the evolutionary supremacy of white people and advocated using eugenics to decrease the population of people belonging to "a low and degenerate race."

At this time in American and European history, eugenics was widely considered a scientifically advanced way to improve the complexion of

---

[1] H. L. Mencken, "Battle Now over, Mencken Sees; Genesis Triumphant and Ready for New Jousts," *Baltimore Evening Sun*, July 18, 1925, https://tinyurl.com/yc73665p.

society. Thirty-two U.S. states had federally funded programs to sterilize men and women within "undesirable" populations—including many who were poor, immigrants, people of color, unmarried mothers, and those who were diagnosed (often wrongly) as being mentally or physically disabled. Eugenics "wore the mantle of respectable science."[2] Hitler studied American eugenics policies and then proceeded to make eugenics infamous forever. This buried chapter of history has only recently received fresh attention.

In sum, though the *Scopes* trial is often used to ridicule fundamentalism, it serves equally as a cautionary tale on the limits of modern science. In the name of science, teenagers were learning some horrendous ideas.

Since then, what has changed? First, scientific support for eugenics has declined to nil (though interest in gene editing has exploded, with all sorts of positive and negative potentials). Meanwhile, public support for teaching evolution has increased gradually but significantly, though the majority of fundamental and evangelical Christians in the United States still oppose it.

This opposition has its work cut out. Today, people who reject neo-Darwinian theory must persuade their audience not only that evolution is unbiblical but also that it is unscientific. By naming what they do "creation science," these Christians acknowledge that science is now the lingua franca of public debate. Mainstream scientists may scoff that creation science is no science at all, but we don't want to miss a larger point: since the time of the *Scopes* trial, science has become our unrivaled public test of truth. When we are We the People, we look at the world through the eyes of science. The People as a whole have no eyes of the heart.

This situation can cause internal tension for believers, extending well beyond debates over evolution. On the one hand, I feel the language of faith, and especially of the Bible, holds the deepest truths of my life. On the other hand, I may feel pressured to defend this truth in public by fitting it into a modern scientific framework instead of drawing from a wellspring

[2] Edwin Black, *War against the Weak: Eugenics and America's Campaign to Create a Master Race*, expanded ed. (Washington, DC: Dialogue, 2012), xvi.

of language and evidence found in the Christian tradition. For instance, a study showing that prayer reduces mental stress becomes something worth bragging about—as if stress reduction were the primary purpose of prayer. Christians in public, if they profess Christianity at all, are less inclined to speak of God than "my faith," since faith is considered a human experience and therefore less offensive to secular sensibilities.

Perhaps to compensate for loss of status, Christians sometimes look for ways to take science down a peg or to put faith and science on a more equal public footing. Just as we saw in the last chapter how scientists in their zeal may distort faith, so we ought now to consider how Christians can fuel conflict by distorting science. Following are three such distortions.

First, believers sometimes portray science as a kind of faith system. Look, a youth minister might say, it takes an awful lot of faith to believe half the stuff those scientists are telling us. When this sort of comment gets inserted during discussions of evolution or the big bang, it sets scientists' teeth on edge.

Yes, some scientists do slide from science into scientism, which is a kind of faith system. And yes, the public accepts on faith things that scientists report, just as scientists do with respect to any field of research other than their own. But overall, scientists are adamant that their knowledge is based on evidence that can be seen and tested. Seen does not necessarily mean eyewitnessed, and testing may not involve repeated lab experiments. But scientists formulated the big bang theory, for instance, by using space to look back in time and by gathering other evidence they could see and test.

Still—it is just a theory, right? To scientists, this comment is equally infuriating. A theory in science is the highest level of explanation, a framework that makes the best sense of all the pertinent facts. Theories are subject to extensive peer review. Theories may be challenged—and usually are—but not belittled. It is never "just a theory," any more than the Christian hope of resurrection is just a hope.

In sum, it is better to teach young people that science and faith are both valid ways of knowing reality rather than conflating the two. If we disparage science by calling it a kind of faith system, then we also disparage faith. The comment cuts both ways. It seems better to say that reality is unified but not uniform: in science, we come to know reality we can see by testing it; in faith, we come to know reality that is unseen largely by living into it.

A second and more obvious distortion occurs when science is portrayed as the enemy of faith. Mentors may tell youth to beware as their impressionable minds enter high school and, much worse, college classrooms, where they can expect their Christian faith to come under sharp attack. Nothing, it is implied, proves the mettle of faith more than a young person's ability to stand against scientific consensus on important issues, such as evolution or evolution or evolution. (The issues may be more than one but not all.)

Removing the bad apple of evolution gets tricky because it is probably the most referenced theory in modern science. Of professional scientists, about 98 percent say humans evolved from earlier life-forms, whereas young-earth creationists believe humans have existed in their present form from the start. While most creationists agree that evolutionary mechanisms can explain change within "kinds" of organisms, they don't accept that one kind can evolve into another—which for Darwin was precisely the point of the whole process.

The young person who has come to accept that mainstream scientists are so flatly wrong at the foundational level of evolution may in time come to believe that scientists are also deceived in some other areas, such as climate change, vaccinations, or genetically modified organisms—which some creationists would say is precisely the point of their educational process. Skepticism of science is meant to translate into more trust of the Bible.

Skepticism has long been considered a virtue within science itself, provided it leads to disciplined investigation. Likewise, conflict can be healthy, since it binds energy to a problem and propels investigation. The young person who is taught in church to reject neo-Darwinian evolution may come to take a more active and studious interest in the subject. By contrast, most young adults are as uninformed about evolutionary biology as they are unconflicted. Sociologist Jonathan Hill found in his research that most young people adopt a position on evolution not by examining evidence but as "a symbolic gesture to indicate to others where they belong in the socio-political landscape."[3]

Overall, though, portraying mainstream science as the enemy to faith has serious pitfalls. It puts a lot of pressure on youth if they must constantly defend their sectarian science against the public truth of mainstream science. Some may withstand this pressure by limiting their range of study and conversation or by maintaining a tightly compartmentalized mind. But the stakes are high, and some will cave in. The young person who has decided that Christian teachers were so flatly wrong at the foundational level of creationism may also in time conclude they were equally wrong on other topics, such as the virgin birth or resurrection or existence of God—which Satan would probably say is the whole point of *his* process.

Christian faith makes many claims that fall outside the bounds of science. It claims, for example, that God exists prior to and independent from all physical matter. But when making claims that do fall within the scientific range, we need to exercise care. If we plan to tell young people that the Bible opposes a theory of which nearly all scientists are certain, then we ought to be equally certain that we are reading the Bible rightly on this issue. Thus far in history, the church has never successfully opposed scientists on matters that are scientific. Thankfully, the history of interaction has been harmonious overall, though not without problems of distortion and miscommunication, as we have just discussed. But there is still another problem to confront.

---

[3] Hill, *Emerging Adulthood and Faith*, 57.

CHAPTER 7

Faith Alone?

C alling science a faith system is one distortion that fosters conflict. It is better to help youth relate but not conflate science and faith. Portraying science as the enemy to faith is a second distortion. Though the enemies narrative has been proclaimed by some modern scientists and perpetuated by some Christians, history is on our side when we tell youth that faith and science are complementary, not competing, paths to knowledge.

We come to a third problem—called fideism (or faith-ism). Just as scientists can slide from science into scientism, so faithful people can slide from faith into fideism.

Sola fide—faith alone—was a famous Reformation slogan, still well known to Protestant seminarians today. *Sola fide* means people are saved by faith in God's grace, not faith plus good works or faith plus human reason. For Luther and other Reformers, grace referred to God's presence and activity in Jesus Christ. Faith was a person trusting and clinging to Christ. Thus faith alone meant Christ alone. The deeper source of salvation is Christ's faithfulness, not the psychological trust or cognitive beliefs of sinful Christians. In sum, the Reformers held a vivid sense of both Christ's goodness and humanity's fallenness.

Borrowing from Augustine, Luther had described sin as *homo incurvatus in se*, humanity curved in on itself, and the Reformers extended this idea into a critique of human reason. Sin darkens the mind and clouds our reasoning ability. Human efforts to know reality, whether through ancient philosophy or modern science, were considered untrustworthy, especially compared with revelation—*sola scriptura* being another oft-repeated Reformation slogan. Since scientific reasoning uses facts, it may appear immune from deception, but this appearance is itself deceiving. Facts mean nothing without theories, and theories are always formulated by human minds, and human minds are always clouded by sin. This way of thinking about thinking influenced Western intellectual history, making doubt a perpetual parasite of human knowledge. However, none of these cogent ideas about the excellence of faith and deficiency of reason takes us all the way to fideism.

Yet what exactly is fideism? Nobody really knows, because theologians apply the word to such a wide array of people and ideas. In this context, I am using fideism as the counterpart to scientism so that scientists and Christians can be said to face corresponding temptations. However, I would like now to distinguish between two basic kinds of fideism: the good kind and the bad kind.

A good version of fideism would assert that a mystical experience can provide direct knowledge of reality. You know, but you cannot say how. You cannot give rational reasons or explanations. You simply know. Pascal said, "Le cœur a ses raisons que le raison ne connaît point" (the heart has its reasons that reason cannot know). I agree with Pascal, though he is sometimes called a fideist. Pascal was also a brilliant scientist, the pascal being a unit of measurement in physics named after him. When Pascal said the heart has its reasons, he was not opposing scientific reasoning but rather pointing to times when we apprehend reality directly, via the "heart," instead of going through a process of rational deduction or induction.

Many people grasp this distinction between these two ways of knowing, even if they can't explain it. But the larger point is that the two ways of knowing—direct reason versus inductive or deductive reason—can be seen as complementary, not competing. However, there is another kind of fideism (which I call the bad kind) that does pit faith against reason. Reason is then portrayed as the adversary of revelation, the impediment to trusting God's Word.

Obviously cases against reason cannot succeed solely on rational grounds—or on scriptural grounds, for that matter. "Come now, let us argue it out" (Isa 1:18)—let us argue it out, says the Lord to Israel, an invitation that propels the ancient Jewish legal profession. Likewise, the revelation of Paul's letters contains numerous instances of complex reasoning. The Reformers wrote extensive logical arguments to defend their position of "faith alone."

Since rational attacks on reason tend to be self-defeating, the argument for this second kind of fideism proceeds by degrees of insinuation. Are we saved by reason or faith? Faith, clearly. And starting in the garden, doesn't human reason lead people into sin? Yes, bad reasoning can lead us astray—as teenagers can attest, since their brain development favors hyperrationality (a decision to get drunk and go joyriding after the prom is usually rationalized). So then, if reason tells you to disbelieve something in the Bible, which one are you going to trust—human reason or God's Word?

The right answer for Christians is always to trust God's Word. But the right question is this: How do we know our interpretation of the Bible is really God's Word? As we see in the Jerusalem Council (Acts 15) and subsequent ecumenical councils, Bible reading always employs human reasoning. We pray for illumination, asking the Holy Spirit to guide our reasoning, not circumvent it. And today, science can be part of the praying, reading, and reasoning process. The Bible itself lifts up the value of observation. As evidence of Christ's resurrection, Paul notes that Jesus was seen by more than five hundred people at one time, adding that most of them are still alive (1 Cor 15:6), in case any skeptics want to go and interview them. John, in the epistles, assures people he is not just fabricating tales but is reporting what he and others have verified with their own eyes, ears, and hands (1 John 1:1).

Like Paul and John, scientists today want to observe and verify, and like scientists, Christians want to analyze and make sense of what we read in the Bible. When we read the Bible, the science of our day invariably comes into play when we are deciding whether to read particular words as poetry or hyperbole or empirical fact. One radiant and oft-cited example is the shape of the earth and its movement around the sun.

In Revelation, John sees "four angels standing at the four corners of the earth" (Rev 7:1). By the Middle Ages, virtually all scholars knew the earth was a sphere, not flat with four corners, and they even knew the earth's approximate circumference. Given their scientific knowledge, they read "four corners of the earth" as poetic image, not empirical fact.

But people in the Middle Ages knew much less about the earth's movement. The Bible says the earth is established by God and it cannot be moved (1 Chr 16:30; Ps 93:1; Ps 104:5). This immobility they took to be a firm fact. The Bible even appears to explain the mechanics of the earth's immobility when it says, "The pillars of the earth are the Lord's, and on them he has set the world" (1 Sam 2:8). When Copernicus presented good evidence that the earth was actually in motion around the sun, his discovery was met with ridicule. Martin Luther is reported to have called Copernicus a fool, saying, "There is talk of a new astrologer who wants to prove that the earth moves. . . . Nevertheless, as Holy Scripture tells us, Joshua bid the sun to stand still and not the earth."[1] These words come from his *Table Talk*, so we are getting them secondhand. But even if inaccurately reported or said in jest, the words express how people thought.

We might suppose Luther was simply going to the Bible and drawing conclusions from a plain reading of the text. But he and other intelligent people drew one conclusion when they read about the four corners of the earth (poetic image) and another when they read that the earth is fixed on its pillars (physical fact). The deciding factor in both cases was the science of their day. The ancient Greeks had learned the earth was spherical, but Aristotle had thought the sun and planets moved around the earth, and Aristotle was still considered a top-notch scientist. When asserting the earth's immobility, theologians were quoting the Bible but thinking of Aristotle.

In other words, this belief in the earth's immobility was not based on the Bible alone but on the Bible plus science. Though the phrase "Bible plus science" sounds like an insult to *sola scriptura*, no one is saying

---

[1] Martin Luther, *Table Talk*, quoted in John Lennox, *Seven Days That Divide the World: The Beginning According to Science and Genesis* (Grand Rapids, MI: Zondervan, 2011), 17.

you need science for salvation or even need science to read the Bible. You only need science when you are reading the Bible and trying to figure out which parts are meant to be scientific. We should add "meant by the Holy Spirit." Even if the writer or first readers of Revelation thought the earth literally had four corners, we are not required to think so, once the Holy Spirit has shown us, via science, that the earth is a sphere.

In other words, we are permitted to bring more science to our reading than the original authors did to their writing. Some of these writers, says Peter, knew that their words would take on new meaning in later generations (1 Pet 1:10–11). Peter has in view the new meaning of fulfilled prophecies, but the unifying idea is this: the biblical words are fixed, yet their meaning is dynamic and not static. The meaning is in motion around the Holy Spirit. Jesus affirmed that the law cannot be altered by one dot, and in the same sermon, he gives people a dynamically new reading of what the law actually means.

A special note is in order for churches with doctrines of biblical inerrancy and infallibility. There is no reason to fear discussing science with youth on this account. There is no need to alter inerrancy doctrines due to science or even to add an asterisk that says, "Use of modern science will void this infallibility guarantee." The only asterisk required is the one already implicit in every official doctrine. For example, the Chicago Statement on Biblical Inerrancy says, "We affirm that canonical Scripture should always be interpreted on the basis that it is infallible and inerrant."[2] The key word in this sentence is not *infallible* or *inerrant* but *interpreted*.

It would be a bad interpretation, as the statement goes on to say, to read as scientific fact something the Holy Spirit intends as poetic image. The statement proposes we should discern the difference between fact and poetry through "grammatico-literary exegesis, taking account of its [the Bible's] literary forms and devices." Here is precisely where science comes into play, whether we realize it or not. To people living post-Copernicus, the phrase "the earth is fixed on its pillars" sure sounds like a literary

---

[2] "The Chicago Statement on Biblical Inerrancy" (Dallas Theological Seminary Archives, 1978), https://tinyurl.com/yapyaha7.

device. But to earlier readers, it sure sounded like a mechanical device, used to ensure immobility.

Where does all this leave us with regard to youth ministry?

First, it shows us that fideism or faith-ism of a particular kind (the bad kind) can fuel conflicts with science. We can chart the movement to this kind of fideism. Faith, which begins as the best way to know God, becomes the best way to know everything—because, it is decided, whatever we need to know in life and death will be revealed to us by reading the Bible. We can be people of one book, as John Wesley professed to be at one point in his life. This position overlooks how much other knowledge we import into our Bible reading, but that's okay. It is still a position of humility, and God gives grace to the humble.

It becomes a position of hubris only when the Christian, in a debate with a scientist, goes on to assert, "I can refute your science with my Bible." The Christian must then endure reproach as various passages are trotted out, such as the ones just discussed, to show how the biblical writers were scientifically inept. "But—but," the Christian replies. "These words are not *meant* to be scientific." Yes; however, we know this fact only because of science. In short, in any discussion of the Bible and science, we must do some science. This point might seem uncontroversial, but it is a point that many church youth might benefit from knowing, and for youth leaders, the preceding discussion may be helpful in understanding why.

Second, bringing science to our reading of the Bible is not the same as basing our reading solely on science. We read through eyes of science but even more through eyes of the heart. Let's picture how this process works in practice. A young person comes to Christ and is given the Holy Bible—an incalculable gift, a paperback or leather-bound object whose contents are fixed and cannot be moved. The canon was settled in the year 367, and the words are established forever. But revolving around the words are human translations that may add or steal meaning, and revolving around the translations are interpretations that reflect, among other things, the science of our day. Nevertheless, a young person given these wonderful words of life is told simply to take up and read—to pray for the inspiration of the Holy Spirit and trust the plain reading of Scripture.

I think this is good advice. The teen who has just found or been found by Jesus may be in a better position to read the Bible through eyes of the heart than many seminary professors I know, myself included. Of course the teen will bring his or her experiences and therefore biases to the text, but we all do that. A gentle reminder, now and then, that the same passage can carry different meanings is usually enough to prompt further learning. As for science, probably our teen knows the earth is round and revolves around the sun, but even if not, she or he will not go horribly wrong in affixing a literal meaning when a poetic one would be more appropriate.

But here is where things do take a turn for worse, even the much worse: when the teen gets into an argument with a scientist about something scientific and then asserts, "Your science is wrong because the Bible tells me so." If I am that teenager, the danger is not that I will lose the argument. The danger is that I will lose my faith after I have lost the argument.

We can avoid this outcome. As a third application of the foregoing discussion, we can teach youth a process of Bible reading whereby we pray and read, then look through eyes of science, then look again through eyes of the heart. Science teaches that there is a contingency from below: people are dependent on physical organs, and organs are dependent on cells, and cells are dependent on molecules. Faith teaches there is a contingency from above: all reality is dependent on God. For Christians, there will be times when we appeal to this higher reality and therefore choose to believe something for which there is no scientific evidence.

This faith is not a superior form of science. It is a conscious, deliberate choice to believe, even when science cannot confirm or explain, even when science can and does view the event as being extremely improbable or logically impossible. At this point, we appeal to God's action from above and to our belief that, for God, nothing is impossible.

This faith is not a denial of science. It includes the hope that science, in exploring contingency from below, will be able to discover hidden harmonies with our contingency from above, thus creating a unity of vision. This faith is not obstinate. It includes the possibility that we and the church may come to reread some feature of our faith in light of further evidence and fresh inspiration of the Holy Spirit. This faith is not fearful. The fact that science has undercut the pillars of the earth does not mean it will whittle away every last pillar of faith.

We will need to be more specific with our youth. They will be looking for a list of things Christians believe that run counter to current science. For most churches, the creeds, if actually believed, provide such a list. However, it could be good to involve youth in a discussion where together we share the events of faith that are near and dear to our hearts. For many parents and pastors, a short list would include the virgin birth, the resurrection, the descent of the Spirit at Pentecost, the miracles of loaves and fish, and the parting of the Red Sea. For some, the list would include every conceivable or inconceivable miracle; for others, the list would be considerably shorter. Some, though I am not among them, would be willing to give up everything but the resurrection, and some even that.

In general, I try to hold in tension two ideas. If God can do one humanly incomprehensible thing (such as, well, exist in the first place), then two or more does not increase the degree of difficulty. There is no need for the list to be short. But at the same time, it does not dignify God's omnipotence when people appeal to it at every turn. If God wanted, someone might possibly argue, don't you think God could have turned the earth from a sphere into a square at the precise moment John saw angles standing at the four corners of the earth, then pushed it right back into a sphere? Don't you think God could do that? Yes, if God can do anything, then that would be something God could do. But God could also be asking you to change how you read the Bible, and given how some minds operate, this result might even be the greater miracle.

Since we are now in the thick of actual interaction between science and faith, it's time to say more about the pattern and process this book is proposing. We can start with what I am *not* proposing. A popular science writer of the last century offered a way to relate faith and science that sounds reasonable, has become widely accepted, and is, I think, fairly wrong.

CHAPTER 8

All Things

To avoid conflicts between faith and science, some scientists and theologians propose that we implement an established principle of modern economics: division of labor. Let faith and science each do its job.

Polls indicate that this idea makes sense to many people. When asked whether science and religion are often in conflict, most say yes. But conflict drops significantly when people are able to give more than a yes or no response. Many people opt for a third choice of saying science and religion do not overlap, since "science is about facts and religion is about values."[1]

In the last century, the scientist Stephen Jay Gould became the primary advocate of this non-overlapping view. Gould coined the term NOMA (non-overlapping magisteria) to say that science and religion are different kinds of inquiry with different domains of teaching authority (magisteria). Gould said science provides reliable facts, whereas religion offers values and meaning. Science gives us the age of rocks; religion, the Rock of Ages.[2] We can feel the appeal of his proposal. When an atheist scientist misrepresents Christianity or a preacher misrepresents science from the pulpit, we may think how nice it would be if some people could just mind their own

---

[1] Jonathan Hill, "Do Americans Believe Science and Religion Are in Conflict?," Big Questions Online, April 6, 2015, https://tinyurl.com/y9w5gabd.
[2] Stephen Jay Gould, *Rocks of Ages: Science and Religion in Fullness of Life* (New York: Ballantine, 1999).

business. A division of labor says we can have mutual respect so long as we have no mutual territory.

The proposal seems to work in practice for some churchgoing scientists. But it can never work in theory—that is, for faith and science as a whole or for scientists who take a more serious interest in faith. The latter tend either to become atheists or else to commence, like Polkinghorne and Peacocke, to look actively for areas of overlap. A division of labor is untenable because science and faith are not just two jobs, like plumbing and electricity, but two ways of seeing everything.

Christianity asserts facts as well as values. Jesus not only taught the Golden Rule, he also made claims about God's energy and activity in the universe. He became the Rock of Ages only after believers declared his resurrection from death to be the central *fact* of the universe. Gould's plan succeeds only if we first strip Christian faith of all unscientific-sounding or miraculous content and then turn it into an ethical system, at which point Jesus becomes one of several potential role models. But classic, orthodox Christianity is not willing to give up its factual claims.

Likewise, science deals with values as well as facts. Though modern scientists do not deal with religious "why" questions, they still make numerous value judgments. They assess what topics are good to research and what methods are good to use. They place a high value on science as a whole and advocate teaching it in public schools. They appear before medical and experimental ethics boards to defend their values. The reclusive scientist, toiling away quietly toward some new discovery, may appear to occupy a morality-free zone. But one discovery usually leads to another, and so it comes to pass, after the explosion of the first atomic bomb, that Robert Oppenheimer is led to exclaim, "The physicists have known sin."

It's true that people specialize. Christian preachers do not usually weigh in on particle physics any more than physicists try to exegete the Greek New Testament. Division of labor also pertains to subfields as well; particle physics is mystifying to most other scientists. But these practical divisions arise from time constraints and personal interests. They do not spell a logical division between faith and science overall because faith and science as a whole both disregard borders, boundaries, or territorial claims.

In short, both Christian faith and modern science drive toward totality. This expansive scope applies to Christianity and not to every ancient or New Age religion. Some "spirituality" can indeed best be described as an activity that people do to gain a boost of power or control. Spirituality in these cases is like an extra layer of life that can be put on or peeled off. But this description cannot, or at least should not, fit Christianity.

From the start, believing in Jesus summoned his followers to complete conversion and an entire way of life. They did not think this way because some became martyrs. Rather, some became martyrs because they already thought this way. Christian faith shaped the whole of life in ways that ran against the grain. Christians rejected the Roman gods and were called atheists. They rejected worship of Caesar and were branded anarchists. As Arthur Darby Nock has noted, Christianity threatened the empire in a way that the ancient mystery religions did not. You could be a Mithraist on the side, but you could not be a Christian on the side.[3] The same is true today: you cannot be a Christian on the side, at least not according to the New Testament.

Jesus is not just an accessory or supplement to life but intends instead to become its center and totality—this according to his own words: every day his followers are to take up their cross; their entire lives are to be yielded to him (Luke 9:23–24). Likewise, Christ in the New Testament letters is not depicted as standing apart from the universe and its scientific operations but rather as intimately involved. He existed before all things, all things were created for him, all things cohere in him, in all things he is to have preeminence, and by him all things are being reconciled to God (Col 1:15–19). This "all things" perspective is found across the theological spectrum. Today's progressive and conservative Christians may differ sharply on their agenda for the Christian life, but both groups hold that this agenda is complete, affecting all of life and every area of life.

---

[3] Arthur Darby Nock, *Conversion: The Old and the New in Religion from Alexander the Great to Augustine of Hippo* (Baltimore: Johns Hopkins University Press, 1998).

Herein lies the rub. With slight modification, the same thing can be said about the agenda of modern science and technology.

Science and technology do not have a set of books comparable to the New Testament, but if we look at what their disciples do, we can learn a lot. We see an impulse toward totality. In physics, scientists search for a "theory of everything," a unifying framework that can explain all aspects of the physical universe—an effort recently directed toward unifying the insights of general relativity and quantum field theory. In biology, some scientists believe they have already found a theory of everything, at least everything organic, in the theory of neo-Darwinian evolution. In this view, humans are basically gene-reproducing machines. Art and music, love and marriage—all things originate and all things cohere because they are tied, directly or accidentally, to genes that confer survival benefits.

Whether the particular theories are right or not, the impulse is the same: science seeks to know everything about the physical universe. Does this desire for total knowledge circumscribe an entire way of life, as Christianity has done? The answer depends on where science leads.

Science in the Christian world begins in wonder and can end there. I see a river of water, so I wonder about water. What is the river's source, and the source of its source, and the Source of all things? But science can also lead to technology, and technology usually leads to more technology, ad infinitum. I see a river of water. I wonder how I can build a dam . . . a water mill . . . a light-water nuclear reactor . . . a heavy-water nuclear bomb.

Nobody can be anti-technology, because technology has been with us since the first wheel and the first fire. Technology takes the knowledge of science and applies it to manipulating the physical world. The difference is not just theory versus practice. Science tends to be more open, technology more bounded. When people in science make a discovery, they write papers and share it with the community. In technology, they hire a lawyer and get a patent. But together, science and technology do touch every area of contemporary life. In tandem, they have created not just knowledge but a way of life, whereby we have attained a high degree of control over our physical environment. Yet paradoxically, many young people feel their own lives spinning out of control.

What happens when technology controls them—and the rest of us? For all its potential goodness, social media technology so often fails to foster true intimacy. Instead, a person can become more machine-like and automatic in responding to stimuli (tags, likes, emojis, etc.) that cause self-esteem to crest or plummet. We create gods and then become like the gods we create, just as the psalmist predicted (Ps 115:8).

The gods of technology do not supply meaning to life, but they do grant ceaseless busyness and entertainment, making it possible to defer questions of ultimate purpose nearly indefinitely. Traditionally, the end of life, in death, forces religious questions to the fore, but even physical death is considered conquerable by technological means, as "transhumanists" speak of the soon-coming day when, as previously mentioned, people will be able to achieve "immortality" by uploading their brain neurons onto computers.

Here then we come back to the biggest problem regarding faith and science. So far, we have been discussing why faith and science certainly ought to interact: to correct the exaggerating tendency of faith and the reducing tendency of science. So far, we have been dealing with problems that arise when faith and science do interact, such as the problem of science turning into scientism or faith into fideism. Interaction is bound to bring some problems and conflicts, but that's okay. They can be addressed. Conflicts at least point to an active relationship.

The greater problem, however, is separation and isolation. The greater problem is non-interaction. Most young people see little to no conflict between faith and science because they see little to no connection. Lack of conflict points to lack of contact. Faith and science each seek to encompass all of life, but they do not encompass each other. Each pursues its path without the other's help. When, on occasion, faith and science do intersect over hot topics, the result is often more heat than light. But most people are not personally agitated.

Through the eyes of science and technology, I see one sort of universe; through the eyes of faith, another. The universes of science and of faith seldom clash. They run parallel. For many young people, this is where the problem really lies: trying to live as one person in two parallel universes. There is no GPS to navigate both at the same time.

CHAPTER 9

A Fate Worse than Conflict

To form a coherent worldview, young people need help relating faith and science. The disconnection between science and faith affects all of us but is particularly acute for youth because they are forming a view of themselves and life in general. Adolescence is a prime time for conversion, passionate devotion, and total commitment to a cause. Therefore, it is also a necessary time to help youth figure out these two most powerful forces in their lives—the spiritual and the scientific.

Though the problem of disconnection between faith and science often goes undiagnosed, we can spot symptoms. By his second year of college, James had become an agnostic. For a period of time before college, he was active in his Presbyterian youth group. The youth pastor was someone he could talk to when his parents were going through a divorce. Gradually, James became intently focused on Jesus.

He recalls the thought that occurred to him one day: "If everything my church is saying about Jesus is true, then we should just drop everything and do this." James was feeling the call, the pull to a total way of life with Jesus at the center. But he looked around at people in church. Clearly, Jesus was not at the center of their lives but more on the periphery. Instead of dropping everything, James decided to drop church.

We can accuse these adults of hypocrisy, but this charge may not stick. What if the adults were actually people of integrity, but their problem was that they were trying to live two separate lives of integrity—one situated in the universe of faith, the other in a universe governed by rules of science, technology, and industry? Let's say I live and work in Washington, DC. On Sunday, I hear that nothing matters more than loving God and loving my neighbors. I fully agree. On Monday, I am told that nothing matters more than widespread economic prosperity and a strong national defense. I could not agree more. These two thoughts are embedded in two thought-worlds, two worldviews, two ways of looking at life as a whole. The two may not necessarily conflict, but they also do not easily connect.

In casual conversation, someone says, "You really should take that trip to Hawaii. After all, you only go around once in life." Or in serious conversation, someone says, "We really must take better care of the earth. After all, it's the only home we'll ever have." A Christian may experience internal pressure because these statements make perfect sense in one universe but are totally wrong in another. In a Christian cosmos, we could go to Hawaii, and we should care for the earth, but our reasoning would refer us back to Christ and to the hope of life beyond the grave, even the hope of a new heaven and new earth (Rev 21:1).

When ideas, information, and images are all swirled together, it makes the problem of non-interaction harder to spot. On their devices, young people see science and religion juxtaposed on the same digital feeds. Cyberspace knows no division between Sunday and Monday worlds. But infinite information only increases the problem of having no adequate way to make sense of it all. Science and faith, though once conjoined, are now pulled apart into two thought-worlds. Even if all things coexist in cyberspace, it is hard for young people to see how the two worlds cohere and harmonize in their minds.

Behind this separation of faith and science, we find a frame of mind based on *naturalism* and *secularism*. If we use too many "ism" words with youth, they will get lost in abstraction, but these two—naturalism and secularism—are good to understand. Naturalism is an outlook that says there is a natural universe and nothing beyond: no God, no life after death, and no special difference between humans and other species.[1] Naturalism takes a scientific focus on the physical world and spins it into an entire worldview. In naturalism, all reality results from physical interactions.

A naturalism worldview easily feeds into a secular way of life. Secularism says we should focus on what is physical and on what is here and now, rather than concerning ourselves with what is hereafter or with what lies above and beyond the material sphere. The secular mind is not seeking a sense of God's presence in the daily routines of public life and, for the most part, not trying to find God in private life either.

Secularism has become an important topic in youth ministry, so it will help to distinguish three meanings of the term. First, secular can refer to the temporal or earthly sphere. In the Middle Ages, the word *secular* was first used to describe monks who left monasteries and priests who ceased doing clerical work in order to return to the mundane world. Second, secular can refer to a public space or epistemological standpoint that is not religious. In the Enlightenment phase of modernity, democratic governments began to mandate neutral public institutions (such as public universities and schools) where all religions were to be equally allowed or equally disallowed.

But *secular* has a third meaning, which is most pertinent to our present discussion. Secular can refer to an entire society or epoch of history in which belief in God is seen as optional and also contestable. In the post-1960s phase of modernity depicted by people such as Peter Berger, James Turner, and Charles Taylor, it is said that a "sacred canopy" no longer stretches over communal life. The common sacred canopy has been replaced by what Christian Smith calls individual "sacred umbrellas."[2] Each person decides for him- or herself whether and what to believe. There was a time, not too long ago, when disbelief in God was nearly unthinkable. But in the West today, disbelief is quite acceptable, whereas belief is

---

[1] Alvin Plantinga, *Where the Conflict Really Lies: Science, Religion, and Naturalism* (New York: Oxford University Press, 2011).
[2] Christian Smith, *American Evangelicalism: Embattled and Thriving* (Chicago: University of Chicago Press, 1998), 106.

considered optional and contestable, especially in some cultures and sub-cultures. In much of the academic world, for instance, atheism and agnosticism are the default intellectual positions.

Some scholars see this third type of secularism as a positive force aligned to freethinking. Others view secularism as a direct challenge to Christian faith or as a parasite that attaches itself to Christianity, morphing classic Christian faith into a flaccid deism. Still others view secularism as the most recent permutation of Christianity, whereby Christianity molts most of its metaphysics in order to preserve most of its ethics.

For his part, the Eastern Orthodox theologian Alexander Schmemann contended that secularism, in all three senses of the word, is an outgrowth of Christianity. The Christian message proclaiming "fullness of life" liberated ancient people to be less fearful of death and more active in relation to the world, giving rise to secular enterprises.[3] But Schmemann saw secularism as a kind of religion, not the absence of religion, and on this score I think he was right. Secularism is the religion of those who say the only world and only life we can know are here and now. Hence we are compelled to be busy, to be happy, to be useful.

The secular mindset can turn people into consumers who feel driven to produce and consume as much as possible in order to squeeze maximal happiness into their one and only life span. Or the secular mindset can turn us into altruists who strive to produce a better world and more just society. The secular mindset can even lead to critiques of consumerism and a zealous desire to live more simply and sustainably. But the running thread in secularism is the sense that we have only one world and one life, which is here and now. Whatever you plan to do or to become must be squeezed into a few short decades. In this way, a new kind of anxiety and oppression creeps in.

What causes this type of secularism? Many people, including most atheists and agnostics, would point to science. They would say that science leads to technology, which leads to economic prosperity, which leads, as

---

[3] Alexander Schmemann, *For the Life of the World* (Crestwood, NY: St. Vladimir's Seminary Press, 1965), 100.

day follows night, to religion's demise. However, James Turner and then Charles Taylor have both made good arguments that science is not really the main cause of secularism. Instead, they contend that secularism came from changes within the church. Says Turner, "Religion caused unbelief."[4] As one development, churches over the centuries turned Christianity into a set of social principles and ethical values that people sought to enact through human effort, without an active sense of God's power and presence suffusing daily life.

Though secularism emerges from Christianity, science can be a contributing factor, insofar as the worldview of naturalism and lifestyle of secularism both lean on science as the basis of knowledge. Both scientist and secularist see a world that can be reduced to physical matter and motion. But for scientists, this world is simply where they work, whereas for secular people, it is where they live and move and have their being.

In sum, while there does seem to be a logical connection between a naturalism worldview and a secularism way of life, science is not the driving force. Yes, scientists do report lower levels of religious belief than the population at large. Maybe they start out that way, or maybe their work shapes their thinking. But people can do good science without embracing naturalism and secularism overall. They can be scientific and Christian at the same time, and the better for it. We see many historic and living examples of this fact.

Saving the rest of this discussion for another day, let's return to the problem of estrangement between faith and science. It should be clear by now that I think a division of labor between faith and science is not the solution but actually part of the problem. If there were more interaction, science could benefit from the meaning, purpose, and ethical guidance that faith supplies. Faith may have a tendency to exaggerate, but faith can also amplify, dignify, and swell with value. Faith clarifies what matters most. Instead of asking only, "How can we do this?" purveyors of

---

[4] James Turner, *Without God, Without Creed: The Origins of Unbelief in America*, New Studies in American Intellectual and Cultural History (Baltimore: Johns Hopkins University Press, 1985).

technology could pause longer to ponder, "Why should we do this?" and "What is truly worth doing?"

By the same token, if there were more interaction, faith could benefit from the carefulness, precision, thoroughness, and circumspection of science. Science may have a tendency to reduce and boil things down too much, but science can also press us toward knowledge of which we feel certain, like coal compressed to diamond. And coupled with technology, science gives us the know-how to enact Christian compassion. Instead of only asking why God allows people to suffer, we can use this scientific know-how to relieve suffering the world over and also to address the root causes of violence and oppression.

In sum, increased interaction between faith and science could make scientific pursuits more meaningful, Christian faith more credible, and Christian compassion more doable on a larger scale. There is great value in bringing faith and science together. Conversely, we can see the lurking danger of allowing the rift and drift between them to continue and widen.

CHAPTER 10

Universe-Based Youth Ministry

The danger of separation is that, for young people especially, Christian claims will become less and less credible in a world where science is the public test of truth. Meanwhile, the technology that grows out of science will become more and more viral, with all the fervent activity masking rather than resolving underlying emptiness, loneliness, and lack of purpose.

We need a pattern and a process to help youth see life through eyes of both faith and science. The goal is to help them live coherent, integrated lives, Sunday through Saturday, in a universe of science that is simultaneously the cosmos of our Creator. If we fail to help youth this way, we can expect they will be pulled from the deep things of God by all the busyness and entertainment that science and technology supremely supply. It will pull them as surely as it has already pulled us.

Most people today live as if there were no God, no God-given meaning and purpose, and no hope of life beyond the grave. They live as if naturalism were true. Many of us will confess with our lips that we believe in God and even tell pollsters we are certain of it. We may sing of our faith softly with fingers folded or loudly with arms outstretched on Sundays. But weekday life does not tend to reinforce the facts of our faith. God seems to be little involved or needed in the science-and-technology world we inhabit.

The National Study of Youth and Religion (NSYR) found teenagers overwhelmingly believe in God, but they also believe God does not need to be involved in one's life, unless called upon to resolve a problem.[1] God makes a series of cameo appearances. On most days, the naturalism world feels busy and entertaining enough as it is.

Is this portrait too pessimistic? Certainly the naturalism bubble gets punctured when a friend or family member dies and it becomes unbearable not to believe in a next life. Even when not facing death, a person may be surprisingly touched by God's grace with a power that penetrates the heart and lingers far longer than the experience itself. But the pessimistic portrait does depict a realistic problem that parents and pastors face: youth do believe in God, but they don't tend to act on it. Their lives are shaped much more by science and technology.

This situation suggests we need an approach to youth ministry that is universe based. Admittedly, this idea sounds pretentious. There have been so many "approaches" to youth ministry already—based on family, friendship, spiritual practices, and more. Do we really need yet another approach, based on the entire universe?

The word *universe* is meant to signal that it may be time for youth ministry to turn to the natural sciences. So far, the field of youth ministry, as taught in colleges and seminaries, has paired theology more with the human sciences (sociology and developmental psychology in particular) in order to look at the lives of youth—their niche in society, their notch on the life span. These efforts have been productive. We now have excellent research to help us see what is happening. But it is precisely when we do look and see that it becomes apparent why a worldview or universe-view approach could make sense, alongside whatever approach one currently embraces.

The National Study of Youth and Religion reported that the vast majority of US teenagers call themselves Christians. However, researcher Christian Smith concluded that most youth have unwittingly departed from classic Christian faith in favor of a different belief system, which

---

[1] Christian Smith with Melinda Lundquist Denton, *Soul Searching: The Religious and Spiritual Lives of American Teenagers* (New York: Oxford University Press, 2009), 163.

he dubbed Moralistic Therapeutic Deism.[2] Youth ministry professionals quickly accepted this diagnosis as describing a problem they had long been witnessing. The term for the belief system, shortened to MTD, became a frequent part of professional youth ministry discussions. What does it mean?

In classic eighteenth-century deism, God sets the universe in motion, establishes universal principles and inalienable rights, and then withdraws from human affairs to watch from a distance. But in this newer brand of deism, God is perceived as being selectively engaged. God is available to meet your personal needs and help you feel good about yourself. God is like a divine butler and invisible therapist. In times of trouble, God becomes a cosmic lifeguard.

Whether or not we use the term Moralistic Therapeutic Deism, one thing is clear: most American youth profess to be Christians, but their Christian faith is not full of consequences. Church is a good extracurricular activity, but faith is not the center of their lives. Regarding a solution to this problem, the National Study offered two significant findings.

First, the research makes clear that parents matter most in the spiritual lives of teenagers. The influence of youth pastors and youth groups pales in comparison with that of parents. One might suppose, therefore, that today's parents have fallen down on the job. Parents of yesteryear must have invested much more time and patient care to pass on Christian faith to their progeny. But is this diagnosis correct? Has Christian nurture really declined so steeply? To this day, I am in awe of my father's faith, but for the most part, his hands-on discipleship consisted in putting his right hand on my left knee and telling my ten-year-old body to stop fidgeting during the long sermon. Were yesteryear's parents really more involved in their children's religious lives than parents of today?

In some cases, yes; in some, no; but on the whole, perhaps parenting has not changed so much as science and technology. Science sees a universe that has been exploding and booming for billions of years, all on its own, apparently without needing God, and technology has been giving us

---

[2] Smith with Denton, *Soul Searching.*

the means to live productive, fun-filled lives all on our own, again with no apparent need of God. These are not new developments, but their pace has increased substantially—some would say exponentially—in recent years. The forces of industry also come into play, working to expand both supply and demand and encouraging people to satisfy spiritual desires with material goods. The result can be a lifestyle of compulsive work combined with compulsive entertainment.

In other words, we need to see not just the powerful influence of parents, but also the powerful forces parents are up against in guiding children toward mature faith. Becoming more attuned to the world of science and technology will help parents and ministers respond to doubts and questions that arise when youth see a universe that runs without God, by laws of science alone, and a daily life that runs without God, by miracles of technology alone.

In addition to the importance of parents, a second big research finding further reinforces why it may be time for a universe-based approach to youth ministry. The National Study reported that Mormons and conservative Protestants were two groups that appeared to be bucking the trend toward an individualist view of faith and an instrumentalist view of God. Mormon and conservative Protestant youth were more apt not only to believe, but also to have faith that made an obvious difference. They could better articulate how faith propelled them to live for God and other people, and they could better point to ways that faith had an impact on their daily lives. "Better" did not mean perfect. The distance between these two groups and other teenagers was not vast enough to warrant convulsions of self-congratulation among their respective denominations. But it does merit attention.

Why did conservative Protestant and Mormon teens tend to be better at talking about their faith and better at demonstrating the difference faith makes in their lives? In the cluster of reasons, one common feature was that these youth had a worldview that meshed tightly with their reading of sacred texts. Further, they were able to maintain this view against stiff opposition. Many of them could tell you, for instance, that the universe is young (not billions but merely thousands of years old) and that human beings have existed in their present form from the start. They could tell you this at the same time 98 percent of scientists are telling them they are flat-out wrong.[3] Even after taking high school and college biology courses, these youth usually stay steadfast. They are actually more likely to remain opposed to neo-Darwinian evolution after learning about it in college.[4] It's not that U.S. science teachers are ineffective or that the United States does not value science. Religiously conservative youth in many other countries oppose evolution to an even greater degree.

This wide gap between these youth and most scientists on questions of the earth's age and human origins calls for interpretation. One might jump to the conclusion that we should spend more time warning youth away from mainstream science and the people who practice it, as if science were a kind of alchemy that turns golden faith into base metal.

This interpretation is mistaken, however, because it is not even what conservative Protestants do. Overall, as noted, they are as pro-science as the general public. But when conservative Protestant youth see a conflict between the Bible and science, they pick the Bible. After all, the scientists are just human. They could be wrong. Scientists have been wrong before, and then some new discovery comes along. Maybe they'll discover something better than evolution. In the meantime, you just have to believe the Bible. This seems to be the attitude that these youth hold. We will address later the question of whether you can accept evolution and still be a Bible believer or reject evolution and still be pro-science. But for now, I think the best interpretation of the research is that it speaks to the power of a coherent worldview.

Accurate or not, the worldview of both Mormons and conservative Protestants has coherence; it is not confused and chaotic, like much of adolescent life or contemporary life in general. Right or wrong, a worldview in which everything fits together is going to stand up a lot better than one where diaphanous bits of truthiness are flapping in the wind. For their part, Christian youth who accept evolution have a harder time articulating how God is involved in the process or how humans are different from animals.

---

[3] David Masci, "For Darwin Day, 6 Facts about the Evolution Debate," Pew Research Center, February 11, 2019, https://tinyurl.com/y2lyzjvl.
[4] Hill, *Emerging Adulthood and Faith*, 53.

In short, youth with a coherent worldview tend to struggle with some central ideas of mainstream science, whereas youth who are more receptive to mainstream science tend to have a less coherent outlook along with a less consequential faith.

Not just with evolution, but also in other ways, Mormons and conservative Protestants see a world in which things fits together. Of course, coherence has its hazards. It can lead to rigidity. It may mean that nuance, complexity, and paradox get squeezed out of the picture. The Christian gospel is replete with paradox. Everything should be made as simple as possible—but not simpler. That said, if adults are unwilling to do the hard work of achieving maximum accurate simplicity, then youth are likely to flounder in the face of incoherence. Incoherence also has its hazards. It can lead to diffusion and chaos. In the face of confusion, youth can become much more receptive to authoritarian leaders who claim to have everything figured out.

Life—especially adolescent life in a rapidly changing society—can feel fractured and disorienting. The need for underlying clarity is clamant. A worldview divided against itself cannot stand, and youth trying to live in parallel universes will inevitably feel pulled apart. In the pulling process, most of the gravitational force will be in the direction of the space where they spend most of their time and energy, which isn't inside a church building.

For their sake, as well as our own, we want to bring the physical universe of science and the spiritual universe of faith into some kind of relationality whereby they are distinct yet unified. Though science and faith rely on different premises, different procedures, and different proofs, our lives depend on both. We pray for healing but also take our kids to hospitals. And not just for practical reasons do we want to help youth embrace both faith and science. It is also for the sake of having a fuller vision of reality and deeper appreciation of mystery.

Though science and faith have very different natures, there must be some model that can offer a union of their insights—a union without confusion of their two natures. As we work to discover such a model, we recall that it has already been found. It was given unto us in the form of a Christmas gift.

CHAPTER 11

Chalcedon

onsider the first Christmas—the incarnation—and the subsequent confession that Jesus Christ is fully God and fully human. It must have been mind-boggling for the early believers, since God and human are very different ways of viewing Jesus.

God is unlimited, the Infinite above all infinities, beyond what our eyes can see or minds can know. God is light but uncreated light. God is love but surpassing any human love. God is life—true life, abundant life, life indeed—and this life is fully in Jesus because Jesus is fully God. And fully human.

Humans are finite, limited in time and energy, subject to hunger and thirst, prone to laughter and tears. As the storm was about to rage, Jesus found a cushion for his head and fell asleep on the boat. Later, when awakened by the disciples, he spoke to the wind and waves, and they obeyed. He was God when he fell asleep, and he was human when he commanded the waves, because the confession of faith says Jesus was and is, simultaneously, fully God and fully human.

It took a bit of deliberation to solidify this confession that Jesus is fully God and fully human, two natures in one Person. For evidence, church leaders examined the Scriptures and lived experience of the church. They prayed and reasoned. Their statement of faith found finished form at the church Council of Chalcedon (Cal-*seed*-en or Cal-se-*don*) in 452. There they clarified that the two natures, divine and human, are united but distinct—in "union, not confusion," meaning not mixed or blended together.

This confession is not scientific, nor is it Muslim, Buddhist, or Hindu. It belongs to a Christian frame of mind and Christian sense of reality. At the same time, Christians are called to live in peace with all people (Rom 12:18) and sent out to interact with the world of science and technology, which we have done from the start. The gospel traveled to the nations via Roman roads, an advanced technology based on the latest science of the day, and some of those roads are still in place today.

What, then, does Chalcedon have to do with faith and science?

Søren Kierkegaard, Karl Barth, and other Christian thinkers have been said to possess a Chalcedonian imagination. They took the pattern of Jesus's two natures and applied it to other areas where they wanted to reconcile disparate descriptions of reality. Why not use this same pattern to understand the relationship between faith and science? Just as divine and human are radically different but equally true (and indeed complementary) descriptions of Jesus, so too faith and science can give us different but complementary descriptions of the world in which we live. The person who has taken this tack more than anyone else is practical theologian James Loder. He showed how the pattern of Chalcedon can illuminate the relationality between science and theology.[1]

Clearly, faith and science need to be kept distinct. As noted, they have different objects of desire and different rules for what counts as persuasive evidence. At the same time, faith and science do share common features: a sense of wonder, a drive toward discovery, and a summoning of passion and commitment. Even some patterns of discovery may be similar. Scientists such as Albert Einstein and Max Planck discovered that physical light, when examined closely, behaves as both particles of light and waves of light. These traits appear contradictory but are actually complementary: you need both wave and particle to give an accurate description of light. This scientific pattern of complementarity between

---

[1] James Loder and W. Jim Neidhardt, *The Knight's Move: The Relational Logic of the Spirit in Theology and Science* (Colorado Springs: Helmers and Howard, 1992); James Loder, *The Logic of the Spirit: Human Development in Theological Perspective* (San Francisco: Jossey-Bass, 1998).

wave and particle is similar to the theological pattern of Christ's divine and human natures.[2]

The physicist Niels Bohr was said to have a Chalcedonian imagination, which he may have gotten from reading the Christian theology of Søren Kierkegaard. Bohr formulated a principle of complementarity in science, which says that objects have complementary traits—such as wave and particle, position and momentum, energy and duration. While these properties cannot be observed simultaneously, both are needed to give a full description.

What is being proposed here is that we use this principle of complementarity for relating faith and science as whole. Both are needed to give a full description of reality. In applying this pattern of Jesus's two natures to faith and science, we are focusing especially on the thinking aspect of faith called theology. Theology studies "the deep things of God" (1 Cor 2:10 NIV), while science examines the deep things of the universe. Together they enable us to see both physically and spiritually. When all is fully known, we will behold one cosmos, one reality, just as Jesus is one Person.

A word of clarification: in talking about the *pattern* of Jesus's two natures, we are not claiming that theology has a divine nature. Theology, like science, is a human activity. Our knowledge of God is incomplete. We see a reflection, as in a mirror (1 Cor 13:12), as in a first-century mirror made of polished metal, not glass. In terms of precision and control, science supplies superior knowledge. If you want to span a river, science helps you build the bridge. If you want to go from earth to the moon, science helps you build the rocket ship. If you want to go from earth to heaven, science has nothing to say.

But heaven and hell are very much topics for theology. Theology asks about God but also humanity, about heaven but also earth, about visible but also invisible things, about life but also death and life after death. Natural science deals with natural things. Therefore, theology corresponds to the "divine" in the Chalcedonian pattern because it has a larger frame of reference. Science looks through physical eyes at the physical universe, which is no small thing. But theology, when it arises from a place

---

[2] Loder and Neidhardt, *The Knight's Move.*

of prayer, looks through eyes of the heart at what transcends the physical realm—things that "no eye has seen, nor ear heard," which are revealed by the Spirit (1 Cor 2:9–10).

Theology does not need to feel either superior or inferior in relation to science. Even when theology's assertions seem based on insubstantial physical evidence, still its Source is radiant and pure. Faith is also more than theological words. Faith is clinging to God, even when words fail. But some words and some doctrines have stood the test of time; they consolidate convictions held by Christians around the world, down through centuries. Imparted to young people, these teachings serve to imbue life with order, stability, meaning, and infinitely large purpose.

How could it work in practice—this idea of complementarity between faith and science? Let's say, for instance, that my daughter Abigail comes home from school one afternoon. As usual, I ask about her day. As usual, she deflects with a vague response, then later decides she has something to say: "Guess what, Dad? In biology, we learned about genes. Humans are 98 percent similar to chimpanzees and about 50 percent the same as cauliflower. Suddenly I don't feel so special."

How do I respond to my daughter's interest and concern? I want to affirm the value of the science she is learning but also offer a complementary lesson on faith. I might begin this way:

Yes, Abby, everything in the universe shares similar atoms and molecules. And on earth, as you just learned, all living things share similar genes and DNA. Genetically, humans are closest to chimps and apes. Of course, the human genome has over three billion base pairs, so that still leaves about sixty million differences between you and Curious George.

But the real reason you are special is not scientific. You are my daughter, so in my eyes, you will always be special. More important, can you see yourself through God's eyes? Before the stars were formed, God predestined you to be adopted as his daughter through Jesus Christ (Eph 1:5). Just as the pupils of physical eyes dilate to let in more physical light, I pray that the eyes of your heart will open wider to see yourself as God does. Augustine said God loves each of us as if there were only one of us. That's how special you are.

These are talking points, not an actual script. The main point is that the science of genetics can fit into a Christian frame of mind. If Jesus can unite divine and human natures in his personhood, then we can unite (but keep distinct) the scientific fact of genetic commonality with the theological idea of *imago Dei*, which says humans are created in God's image and likeness (Gen 1:26–27). Can we really be like chimps or cauliflower yet also be like God? Yes. The metaphor for these two ideas is not oil and water but flip sides of the same coin—or better yet, the divine and human *pattern* from Chalcedon, two seemingly contradictory natures united in one person.

What does it mean to say that a compilation of DNA has been created in God's image? Here we turn from science to theology. Christian tradition has interpreted this idea to mean that humans have an honored place in creation, as God's representatives. Humans have a special closeness to God, a Godlike capacity for relationality, and Godlike attributes such as creativity, reason, and love.

This high calling is not incompatible with base origins. My daughter can learn she shares DNA with chimps or cauliflower—and she shares in the image of God. Likewise, the water of baptism is the same water she uses to take a bath—and it is the washing of regeneration (Titus 3:5). The wine of communion is made from the same grapes she pops in her mouth every day—and it is a participation in the blood of Christ (1 Cor 10:16). Jesus himself came into the world as a fully human baby dripping with amniotic fluid. And he is the eternal, immortal, invisible, only wise God. Humanity is formed from dust yet inbreathed with God's Spirit.

What we see may appear lowly and base, but there is more to us than meets the eye. Divine treasure resides in jars of clay. These are Christian paradoxes, though perhaps everyone lives with some kind of similar paradox. (The strict materialist is very committed to the idea of materialism, though both the idea and commitment feel intangible and immaterial.)

That humans are closely connected to all living things and even to molecules of stardust does not need to threaten faith but can illuminate it, especially when conjoined with the conviction that we are able to transcend our carbon-based confines.

In sum, the person of Jesus himself, as described at Chalcedon, gives us the reassurance that we can reconcile the contrasting but complementary insights of faith and science. This reconciliation can be deeper than a mere truce and better than an untenable division of labor. It can enable a fuller, more truthful and life-giving vision of reality. If this is the pattern—Jesus Christ as described by the early councils—then what is the process? What do we tell ourselves, and what do we tell our youth? What we tell ourselves is important because no matter what we tell them, they will sense what we actually believe.

If we fear science, they will sense it. If in our bones we feel the world of faith is less weighty than the world of science and technology, they will sense that too. And so, while it may sound abstract or ethereal, the most practical question for youth ministry is this: What do we believe is really real?[3]

---

[3] A note to those who think philosophically: This book is not trying to solve the mind/body problem or spiritual/material problem at a philosophical level.

Most of us have an everyday intuition that there is something true about monism (namely, the unity of the spiritual and physical realms) and also something true about dualism (namely, the distinction of those two realms). The beauty of the Chalcedonian pattern is that it combines both truths. Jesus, in his incarnation, unifies yet keeps distinct the spiritual and physical realms.

Exactly how he does so, scientifically speaking, is a question to which most Christians don't claim to have an answer. We cannot "figure Jesus out" apart from a decision to become united with him and an endeavor to become like him. Hopefully, however, we don't need to explain the process of the incarnation to benefit from its pattern: the language of science and faith can coexist in our minds (and brains). The two can be kept distinct, yet they become unified because they both ultimately yield knowledge that is good, beautiful, and true.

CHAPTER 12

Home Is Where You Start From

People who go off to college can usually recall, many years later, their first year on campus and the first friends they made. My friends and I bonded around our newfound intellectual interests. Dorm room discussions and debates could stretch for hours into the night.

I soon learned the trick of arguing by questioning premises. Every case about anything is based on some starting place. Question the premise—whether it is the existence of God or the veracity of historical records or the reliability that one's waking state is not actually a dream—and you presume to threaten the argument.

While learning thus to thrust and parry, I was also unwittingly slicing to pieces my own sense of reality. By second year of college, my thinking had induced a head of anxiety. As I walked back from a party one snowy evening, a flood of thoughts came upon me, and soon I was questioning not just abstract premises but my sense of reality and my own existence. Like a cartoon character running off a cliff, I looked down at my feet and saw nothing. This loss of selfhood did not produce Buddhist tranquility but instead a panic attack, followed by a lingering feeling that everything normal had now become uncanny and bizarre.

Some years later, after an experiment in praying, a series of remarkable coincidences reignited my Christian faith. I began to sense again that God was real. Further, I was struck by the feeling that God cared about me personally. Again my sense of reality was being fractured but now in a good way, as in a kaleidoscope when a strange symmetry suddenly appears. I visited a Presbyterian minister to talk about what was happening to me. This minister was also a seminary professor, and during the visit, he gave me a copy of a book he had written on the topic of "transforming moments." It sounded pertinent.

I read his book and took notes, almost a page of notes for every page I read. Then I returned to his office, ready to debate. Wanting to agree with much of what he said, I needed to be sure. I wanted to test his arguments in order to see whether they could withstand the onslaught of my premise questioning. As it turned out, they could not.

At first, he tried to answer my objections. Then I started down a Hamlet path of relativism that says nothing is good or bad but our thinking makes it so, at which point he grew quiet and still. Nodding slowly, he said with kindness and a hint of exasperation: "Okay, if that is what you really believe, then go out and live that way." He was calling my bluff or presenting a choice—saying in effect, "You can start from the premise that nothing really matters or that good and evil are just fictions of the human brain. But it is no idle discussion. Living with integrity means living out our convictions. If nothing really matters, don't suddenly pretend otherwise at the birth of a child."

Faith became a choice that day. We are thrown into life, naked and wriggling, but gradually our eyes open, our senses awaken, and there comes a time when we choose—individually or communally, suddenly or gradually, consciously or unconsciously—the kind of reality we want to see. Yes, there is no premise that cannot be doubted. But you have to start somewhere because you have to live now. Choose this day. I realized something about myself that day. I really and truly wanted to believe. And I could think of no good enough reason not to.

In arriving at the starting place of Jesus, I was returning home to a decision made in childhood. The personal events that brought me to this starting place were personally significant, though I sensed I could have come by other routes. All the gains and losses of adolescence can become part of the road to God or back to God.

From my personal history I drew lessons applicable to discussing faith and science with youth who exhibit intellectual curiosity. First, every premise can be doubted. This is true in science no less than religion. Scientists look for hidden order on the premise that the universe is, in fact, orderly. But this premise can be doubted, and a scientist may wonder from time to time whether the universe is ultimately chaotic, whether orderly theories are just constructs imposed by the human brain.

Second, in both faith and science, our physical senses matter less than the invisible theories and paradigms we hold inside us. To illustrate this second point, consider this exchange between Werner Heisenberg and Albert Einstein. Heisenberg is discussing his observation of electron orbits inside an atom. He tells Einstein, "It is reasonable to consider only those quantities in a theory that can be measured."

It makes sense. We should build a theory on things we can see and measure. Heisenberg assumed this point was obvious.

But Einstein disagrees. "But you don't seriously believe that only observable quantities should be considered in a physical theory?"

Taken aback, Heisenberg replies, "I thought this was the very idea your relativity theory is based on?"

"Perhaps I used this kind of reasoning," Einstein allows, "but it is nonsense nevertheless. . . . In reality the opposite is true: only the theory decides what can be observed."[1]

The theory decides what we can see in the first place. The theory, which we hold inside us, acts as the interpretive framework that filters reality. It is constantly telling us what we are observing. We don't observe reality and then form a scientific theory. Instead, some prior theory—some mental construct of reality—is shaping what we are able to see.

For example, scientists in the 1930s observed what they called "dauer modifications." These modifications in an organism were produced by interaction with the environment and subsequently were passed on to the

---

[1] Tony Fleming, *Self-Field Theory: A New Mathematical Description of Physics* (Boca Raton, FL: CRC, 2012), 201–2. The dialogue inside quotation marks comes from Fleming's book and is a translation from German; the narrative description is my own wording. Cf. Werner Heisenberg, *Encounters with Einstein and Other Essays on People, Places, and Particles* (Princeton, NJ: Princeton University Press, 1983), 10–11.

organism's offspring. Then newer, more "mature" theories of genetics came along that said acquired characteristics cannot be heritable. So scientists stopped seeing dauer modifications. Decades later, theories of epigenetics again changed what scientists were able to observe. It is now believed that the effects of personal trauma, and perhaps other life experiences as well, do get passed on to one's offspring, even to the third and fourth generation.

Here's another, even easier example of how theory shapes what we see. My daughter and I used to watch talent shows on YouTube. When a magician performed an act, we saw the same person, but we observed two different acts due to our two different theories. As white-winged birds appeared and disappeared into thin air, she observed a display of superpowers, whereas my theory told me I was seeing physical props and sleight of hand. Even though my eyes could not actually detect these physical phenomena, I knew very well what I was observing.

Our theories shape the reality we see, which is not to say everything is just a mental mirage. Rather, the mind receives data and then fashions it into orderly form. We participate in composing our sense of reality. The mind that works this way can also wonder from time to time whether it has worked too hard and imposed more order than actually exists. The mind may even wonder whether there is ultimately any order at all or whether anything physical—from orbiting electrons to the technology that produces virtual reality—is really real. In some worldviews, the physical realm is altogether illusory. Culturally, this notion is foreign to us, in part because the God of the Hebrews cares about the physical realm and because Jesus was born of flesh and blood and ate physical fish, even after the resurrection. The material world matters.

To recap: First, our sense of reality rests on premises or starting places, which can always be doubted. Second, from each starting place, we form theories that shape the reality we see; these theories can also be doubted and challenged. But now, as a third point, we tend to have fewer doubts about premises and theories we share with the rest of society. Our sense of reality is communal, and this is true even in individualistic cultures. For example, people in the United States believe strongly in individual freedom in part because it is a communally shared value.

As a society, we work together to compose and maintain our sense of reality. Our current communal reality is physical, scientific, and techno-logic. The public square is paved with concrete. It is no longer populated with invisible spirits, as it was in former times and as it still is in places beyond the Global West. Society-wide, in North America and Western Europe, we publicly affirm physical reality, while spiritual things are rel-egated to some private sphere—inside the church, inside the home, inside your mind.

This shift in our communal sense of reality has also swelled in us a communally shared sense of superiority. The dramatic scientific and economic progress we have made tells us we are much better off than people a thousand or even a hundred years ago. Discounting the damage of postmodern living to our psyches and environment, we are, most of us, very glad to be living now and not in some earlier, more "primitive" era. I am not being snide. I too believe this is the best time on earth to be alive.

Only infrequently do we pause to wonder whether our intense physi-cal focus has occluded our spiritual vision. Just a few centuries ago, the spiritual sparks were flying everywhere. Meaning and numinous pur-pose were located in things themselves, not just in the brain. Spirits lived in trees, and nestling dragons resided in rivers, which is why baptismal waters needed to be exorcised, even as baptismal candidates themselves underwent prolonged exorcism. Invisible spiritual entities, both good and bad, suffused daily life. Outside the Global West, this way of thinking continues. From time to time, one reads reports of Asian technology com-panies hiring Shinto priests to exorcise their software before they install it, to reduce the incidence of demon-induced bugs and viruses.

But in the Global West, spirit and matter got sent their separate ways. Today, the physical universe contains invisible atoms, not invisible spirits. It is possible to imagine a universe where atoms and spirits coexist, but most scientists looking through the telescope or microscope see a despiri-tualized physical universe, as do most people peering into their handheld devices. This despiritualized universe makes sense to us because we can explain it and control it, and we have a communal theory that explanation and control are far better goals than mystery and acceptance.

To be sure, explanation and control are strong motives that propel science and technology forward. Only infrequently do we pause to consider how an explanation can be fully accurate without being truly adequate. And what does it profit us if we are able to control the entire earth yet lose our self-control? Still and all, a despiritualized physical universe is our common ground, science our common truth.

Thus our sense of reality comes from both external stimuli and internal imagination and from both personal decisions and communal heritage. In these pairs, which is more important—the internal or external, the personal or communal? The answer is probably both. We value internal imagination, but an overactive imagination means you are losing a grip on reality. We value communal heritage, but our heritage commends individuals who are able to stand against the stream. With external and internal, it is necessary to have both, and with personal and communal, it is frequently possible to choose both.

Adolescence is often when a young person's communal heritage becomes a personal choice. It is, as the saying goes, when your grandmother's religion becomes your own personal faith. The choice to accept Christ is different from the choice to accept science. Do nothing, and science will still pervade your life, via technology and because it is our public truth. But Jesus stands at the door and knocks, and the knock goes easily unheard amid the din of work and entertainment activity.

Work and entertainment constantly reaffirm reality seen through eyes of science, but reality seen through eyes of the heart is constantly challenged by benign neglect. Once a year, a tree is erected in the public square; once a year, Christmas carols with an updated beat drift through public speakers as background noise for shopping and dining. The National Study of Youth and Religion showed that young people see Christianity as a "very nice thing,"[2] which is not in fact a very good thing. Where there is harsh persecution of Christians, it means the Christian sense of reality is

---

[2] Kenda Creasy Dean, *Almost Christian: What the Faith of Our Teenagers Is Telling the American Church* (New York: Oxford University Press, 2010), 6.

seen as a threat, which means it is seen as real. But in America, persecution takes the form of bad caricatures in the media.

Of course, no one should wish for persecution. Rather, the point is this: because public life in America does so little to reinforce Christian realities and so much to distract from Christian priorities, the church community becomes all the more important in helping children start out with a Christian sense of reality. And because church members do not typically live together, the pressure falls on the household to create an environment that fosters faith.

Many books have been written on this topic of Christian nurture. The family heritage we endeavor to pass on to our children includes the belief that honest questions deserve an honest answer. My wife and I have a theory that our children will be more apt to think we are being truthful about Jesus if they sense we are not in the habit of making stuff up, whether we are talking about faith or sex or Santa Claus.

When our daughter was six, she asked me one night at bedtime, "Is Santa Claus real?"

"No," I said. I then proceeded to explain how there were various legendary persons who gave gifts to children, but with the rise of the bourgeoisie and increased discretionary income in Europe and America, Christmas rose to prominence as a gift-giving holiday, and the imaginary personage of Santa became elevated by mercantile interests. Actually, I told her the first clause of that sentence and kept the rest to myself.

She pondered. "So he doesn't really come down the chimney?"

"No," I said.

I sensed she had previously been on the fence about Santa, and the chimney business was a particular sticking point. We had done nothing to encourage belief in Santa, but we live in a region of the country that has year-round Christmas stores and even a town established in 1853 with the official name Santa Claus. Thus I counseled her against speaking about this matter with her young friends. This advice she promptly disobeyed. The next day, my wife had to deal with the sobs of a neighboring child, as our daughter had suddenly become a destroyer of faith.

But at any rate, we believe Christian faith can grow stronger in an environment of hard questions and reasonable doubts. I think part of

C. S. Lewis's enduring appeal is due to the candid, British commonsense, empirical approach he takes. He is like a converted David Hume. As a literary critic, Lewis knows that many cultures have myths of dying and rising gods, and there is no need to hide this fact from the kids. Instead, this fact gets woven into a positive argument for Christianity as being the myth that actually comes true, with other myths expressing the ingrained universal longings to which Jesus is the fulfillment.

Sooner or later, if our daughter has inherited the mental disposition of her parents, she may have doubts about Christianity. She will have to decide for herself. Jesus will reveal himself to her but not force himself upon her. But the capacity to see through eyes of the heart starts in childhood. At the same time she is learning science and using technology, I want her to know there is more to reality than meets the eye. A completely accurate view of physical reality is still not adequate for living a fulfilled life. We need to help youth see through eyes of the heart.

To illustrate this fundamental point, we could take a printed book, even this book in your hands, if it is printed and not digital. We can describe the book's physical properties in terms of carbon black ink with a slight amount of titanium dioxide, layered onto low-white, wood-free uncoated paper weighing somewhere between sixty and ninety grams per square meter. What else would you like to know about the book? Perhaps we could measure more precisely the weight of the paper or study the surface area ratio of paper to ink. This physical description of a book as black dots on white paper is totally accurate but not at all adequate for a person who has learned to read. For the reader, the carbon black ink and wood-free paper are transformed into words. The words carry invisible meaning, purpose, and power that a dots-on-paper investigation can never disclose.

Learning to read starts in childhood, and it starts by trusting that the black dots mean more than meets the eye. Faith in Jesus can begin much the same way and over time become a way of reading reality, all of it.

People arrive at this starting place by various routes, and the traveler may sense there could be various destinations. But when you truly arrive, you know you are home, and you need look for no other.

CHAPTER 13

Three Conclusions.

K eeping in mind the pattern from Chalcedon, we can draw three conclusions from prior chapters.

First, science and faith look at one reality.

Second, they see it differently, pursuing different questions, drawn by
different desires, weighing different evidence.

Third, their two ways of seeing can be complementary instead of
competing—provided we start with faith. If we give priority to the deep
things of God and cultivate a Christian frame of mind, we are not forcing
religion on our children but instead are introducing them to a way of reading life and death through eyes of faith.

We can say more. The first conclusion—that faith and science behold
one reality—follows from the premise that tributaries of truth lead to the
same sea. If reality is coherent, then perfect science and perfect faith must
one day touch and kiss. This oneness of faith and science is not a numeri-
cal singleness but a unity within relationality. Currently, many young
believers experience reality as twoness. There is a bifurcation between
their personal Christian faith and the public workaday world of science
and technology. Healing this split is the challenge before us.

The second conclusion concerns the road to get there. Currently, science and faith conflict around a few hot topics, but the greater problem
is their overall non-interaction and thus the sense that science and faith

belong to two different universes. Christian youth in an age of science are pressured to live parallel lives. In a curved universe, parallel lines eventually meet—a hopeful metaphor. But we don't need to wait, nor can we afford to. Already we can build bridges and find convergences between faith and science. Starting now we can help youth see how science keeps in check the exaggerating tendency of faith while faith corrects the reducing tendency of science. This kind of teaching requires that we too learn to see binocularly and speak bilingually. If we ourselves can appreciate the complementarity of faith and science, then we have a message to impart.

As an example of this complementarity, recall that science and faith ask different questions. Science starts with the physical universe and asks how things work. Youth can know the answers to more "how" questions than any generation in history. Scientific success is evident in our tremendously increased material production and prolonged human life span. But *why* do we live? What is the meaning of life? Youth are wont to ask these questions too.

Questions of life lead inevitably to questions of death, as surely as night follows day. We live in a "cosmic cemetery,"[1] and death is everywhere apparent, from the cells on our body, which die at the rate of 300 million per minute, to the winding down of the entire universe via entropy. Though death seems to have the last word in the physical universe, Christian faith declares that Christ is risen from the dead, and by God's power, others will likewise be raised. Someone will ask, "But how are the dead going to be raised? What kind of body will they have?" These are good, scientifically minded questions, and faith at this point has no good scientific answer, only imperfect analogies, such as seeds that get buried in the earth and later flower into sheaves of wheat.

Science does not presume to say why we live or die, but science does persist in asking how. The how in science is so paramount that the whys recede from view, and in fact, most why questions get turned into how questions. When a girl asks Dawkins about the meaning of life, he replies,

---

[1] Alexander Schmemann, *For the Life of the World* (Crestwood, NY: St. Vladimir's Seminary Press, 2004), 100.

"Rocks are just here," and so, too, "Life is just here." "Here" can mean anywhere or nowhere. The girl has asked a question that modern science is not able to answer.

Christian faith, by contrast, has the temerity to say that the meaning of life is so simple that even a little child can learn it. Why do we live? To know, love, and serve God in this life and be supremely happy with God in the next (a traditional Catholic answer). What is the chief purpose of life? To glorify God and fully to enjoy God's benefits forever (a traditional Protestant answer). These answers await a host of questions: Then why is there so much suffering? Then why is God so often hidden? Christian faith persists in asking why. The why becomes so paramount that the hows often recede from view.

Theologian James Loder recounts the story of a young woman who, following a broken love relationship, is intent on committing suicide. She decides to clean up her apartment first, so it is not a mess when they find her body. In the process, she comes across an Orthodox icon that her mother had given her. She lights a candle and begins to pray for forgiveness for this thing she is about to do. As she looks into the icon, through wisps of smoke she sees the figures of Mary and Jesus, and through them she sees herself and her life anew. She rises from her knees with new-found hope and resolve to live.[2] How does this transformation happen? It happens somehow. Somehow the love of God is the telic cause behind the physical chain of events. God's love is the why that spans all physical hows.

Not every story of despair ends so happily, and again we could ask why. But her story is consistent with those of other young people who have encountered God. People experience love—both God's love and human love—as palpable forces, though science does not presume to measure this force. To take a hypothetical example, let's say Joe or Jane has a mystical vision. Subsequently, Jane's neurologist discovers a benign tumor in her dorsolateral prefrontal cortex, and the neurologist begins to explain

---

[2] James Loder, *The Logic of the Spirit: Human Development in Theological Perspective* (San Francisco: Jossey-Bass, 1998), 85.

to Jane how such tumors can cause strange mental events such as, well, mystical visions. But the vision has already happened, and whatever its physical roots, its reality has already outgrown the physical realm. And so logically, Jane may reply, "Okay, then I guess God used that tumor to give me the vision." And why not, if God would speak through a donkey or use an instrument of torture to redeem the world? In back of all physical causality, the love of God becomes the final, telic cause.

This notion of double causality is infuriating to nonbelievers, especially if they have a scientific frame of mind. But to many believers, it is how we live in the everyday world of medical science and modern physics, while still inhabiting this other world that feels even more real, more personal, more meaningful. The believer wants to live in both worlds simultaneously, as if they are one and the same, which they are.

Most people are believers in this sense that they want meaning and purpose to be out there in the universe, not just inside the brain. Here's another story, which comes from an obituary in a college alumni journal.[3] A woman named Kim writes about her lifelong friend Julie. Kim and Julie were both in their fifties. They had first met in kindergarten, then became separated, and then suddenly reunited one day at college: "We found ourselves walking toward each other on an empty quad in overcoats. It felt like a Sergio Leone movie. We started talking and never stopped."

After college, Kim and Julie lived together in Los Angeles. On a whim, they decided to go hiking in Nepal, though Julie "was down to half a lung at that point. We struggled at the back of the pack but completed the trek." A short while later, Julie died.

"The day after she died," Kim writes, "a white butterfly landed on my heart and just sat. I said, 'Hi Julie!' She continues to visit me, and I know many share my gratitude for having known her determination, humor, intelligence and acceptance."

The whiteness, shape of the wings, and many other things about the butterfly can be explained in terms of scientific cause and effect. But why on this particular day does a winged creature alight on her heart and

---

[3] Laura Scandrett, "In Memory, Julie R. Engelsman," *Amherst Magazine* (Winter–Spring 2018).

linger? Physical causes could say how it happened, but only how, whereas for Kim the why of this experience points to radiant meaning that suffuses and surpasses the physical realm.

The psychologist Carl Jung coined the term *synchronicity* to describe these sorts of meaningful coincidences, which often occur when a loved one has died and often involve winged creatures. Jung went on to propose that the universe is held together not only by a space-time continuum and physical causality but also by an indestructible energy and meaningful connections. He said these meaningful connections and coincidences are so powerful because they constitute a real ordering force that is out there in the universe, not just in the brain.

People persist in thinking life can have meaning that endures beyond physical death. To pick on Richard Dawkins again, it's worth noting that he begins his book *The God Delusion* with this dedication: "*In Memoriam*, Douglas Adams (1952–2001)." He does not dedicate his book to the surviving DNA of Douglas Adams, which arguably still exists, but rather to the person himself—a person who, in Dawkins's worldview, does not exist. Further, the phrase *In Memoriam* comes from traditional religious burial rituals. Why does the world's all-time best-selling book on atheism begin with this stark remnant of solemn prayer?

Atheists, agnostics, and skeptics may cling to religious roots, and not only from communal habit, but also from some hidden intuitions that life is more than meets the eye, more than its physical dimensions. The indestructible energy of God's love suffuses the universe, even in the face of horrific suffering and horrendous wrongdoing. For my children, I pray the eyes of their hearts will open wider to let in more light.

In terms of its pure physicality—its size, duration, energy, and impact—a human life span of eighty or ninety years is so puny as to be meaningless. Set against the thirteen-billion-year scheme of the universe, our life on earth barely counts as a pre-death experience. From entrance to exit, it is about as physically significant as a gnat hitting the windshield of a speeding car. But faith gives a different reading of reality in which moments suspended in time can become redolent of eternal purpose. Each act of love, no matter how small—a cup of cold water given in his name—has eternal value. A small sparrow's fleeting life, seen through God's eyes, possesses sacred worth (Matt 10:29). Nothing of love is lost along the way.

As a rejoinder, the skeptic may call this faith a form of wishful thinking. The story of infinite, redeeming love may sound too good to be true. But what if it is true and even too true to be good—that is, what if this truth cannot be confined by ordinary bounds of good and evil, such that the evil of the cross becomes transformed into Good Friday and death itself becomes a Passover to fuller life? What if there is barely enough evidence to believe this truth, but then, after some initial, imperfect, yet momentous act of faith, the evidence starts to coalesce and grow as faith leads to more faith?

In her teenage years, Jennifer had some transforming experiences of God's love. As a young adult, she told me why she and her young Pentecostal friends were inclined to interpret, and even overinterpret, physical events as God's handiwork. She used the analogy of post-traumatic stress. A person who has been traumatized at night may have abnormal fears of nighttime noises and may rush to interpret any random sound as impending danger. Jennifer said that something similar, though opposite, can happen when young people experience God's love in a way that overwhelms them and touches the core of their being. The experience guides their subsequent reading of reality. They may rush to interpret any odd experience—a job that suddenly comes through, a traffic stop that results in a warning and not a ticket, a rainfall that starts or stops at just the right moment—as further inbreaking of this same love in their lives.

The exclamation "Look what God did for me!" sounds like narcissism to some people.[4] Sam Harris takes this position. He says it is conclusive proof of narcissism if you think God cares about you personally. But then Harris does not believe in a personal God. Contra Harris, feelings of being personally loved by God can actually help people to grow out of narcissism and into greater empathy and compassion for others. Narcissism

---

[4] Sam Harris, *The End of Faith: Religion, Terror, and the Future of Reason* (New York: W. W. Norton, 2005).

feeds on fears that love is in short supply. Perceiving and receiving the love of God—a limitless river leading to an endless sea—can release a freer flow of love from the small tributaries of one's own heart.

In explaining why she and her Pentecostal friends interpret daily events as signs of God's love, Jennifer reminds us that faith may tend to exaggerate. Science can keep this tendency in check, though we might ask why it even needs checking. Certainly there is no harm and much good in believing that God's love is the final cause of everything or that God is ultimately behind everything we see. This is a faithful way to live. It enables us to say, for example, that the arc of the moral universe bends toward justice.

The problem lies rather in claiming certitude about the path of intervening causes that winds between our present circumstances and God's ultimate purpose of love. While it is good to believe that God acts in specific, identifiable ways, we don't want our faith to turn into presumption. How do we respond to the prophet who claims to know that a particular hurricane, earthquake, or pandemic is God's judgment? To the woman who forgoes medical intervention because she is trusting God to heal? To the man who lacks financial discipline because he is trusting God to provide?

In these situations, we benefit from having a scientific sensibility that looks at empirical evidence and statistical probabilities. This path need not lead to blanket skepticism but rather can serve to refine faith by making it more sober minded (1 Pet 5:8). We can remind youth that God also works through good medical procedures and sound financial planning. Meanwhile, we can also explain how the reducing tendency of science, when extrapolated into an entire worldview, can lead to feelings of futility. When young people vacillate between ideological hunger and pervasive cynicism, it may signal to us that they are oscillating between two parallel universes. By bringing these worldviews into unity, we help them attain a realistic outlook, one that is open to the infinite love of God in their lives.

Realistically, for example, this rising generation can work toward the goal of supplying clean water to every child and family on earth. This project summons scientific knowledge, and we know, scientifically, it can be done. In working toward this goal, they will face innumerable obstacles. Human corruption, selfishness, and greed will be staring them in the face, even at times when they look in the mirror. Yet this they call to mind and therefore have hope: even one cup of cold water given in Jesus's name has eternal value. Science and faith, in this case, are not just complementary ways of seeing reality but urgently needed partners. We need science to survive but faith truly to live.

CHAPTER 14

Why Faith First?

The third conclusion offered in the previous chapter describes the order in which faith and science can fit together in our thinking. Starting with childhood teaching, it is best to begin with faith and then add science. But why? An analogy helps answer this question, and again the analogy comes from Chalcedon.

If we start with the humanity of Jesus, there is no way to reason our way up to his divinity. No rabbi in his right mind would say, "I and the Father are one" or "Before Abraham was, I am." Humanly speaking, these claims are blasphemous, and Jesus's first listeners were understandably perplexed. Even a worker of wondrous miracles would never claim equality with God, for only God is equal to God. Thus in the classic Christian narrative, the order of logic begins with Christ's divinity—with the incarnation and with the Spirit's revelation that Jesus is, as Thomas declares, "my Lord and my God."

Starting with Jesus's divinity, we can fit his humanity into this framework: Jesus demonstrates what it means for a person to become truly and fully human, as God intends humanity to be. We too can do the works Jesus did, by the power of his Spirit living in us (John 14:12). We too can be partakers of the divine nature (2 Pet 1:4), participating in the energies (though not the essence) of God. As Athanasius stated so memorably: God became human so that humans could become like God. This is the

Christmas story we retell each year. God was born of our flesh so that wecan become born of God's Spirit.

Now to apply the analogy: starting with science is like starting with the humanity of Jesus. No scientist in her right mind would assert Christian convictions in a scientific journal, for such statements sound like blasphemies against the canons of modern science. Science focuses completely on the material realm, whereas faith turns its gaze to the immaterial. The scientist looks for principles and patterns that are impersonal, whereas faith makes everything personal. The scientist wants to achieve maximum clarity, but faith speaks of mystery as if it were a good thing. The scientist tries to analyze phenomena into basic components, thus to explain the complex in terms of the simple, whereas faith appears to explain the complex in terms of the inscrutable. God's ways are not our ways, so how can we possibly fit them into scientific terms? At the outset, God's very name—I Will Be What I Will Be (Exod 3:14)—declares that every scientific paradigm will fail to explain the phenomenon at hand. Starting with science and trying to think our way into faith is like starting with the humanity of Jesus and trying to reason our way up to his divinity.

Modern science intentionally excludes reference to divine action. Pierre Laplace presented to the emperor Napoleon a system of physics in which every action and event in the universe is determined by fixed and impersonal physical laws. Napoleon asked, "Where does God fit into your system?" Laplace replied, "I have no need of that hypothesis."

The story is apocryphal, and the strict determinism of Laplace's system has since been undermined by quantum physics. But Laplace's sentiment abides among scientists. Nowhere in any peer-reviewed scientific journal is anything explained in terms of divine activity. They have no need or desire for that hypothesis. Within a scientific framework, one will wait in vain for some gap in knowledge that causes the scientist to exclaim, "Surely the presence of the Lord is in *this* place!" The instruments of modern science were never designed to detect God.

But if our order of logic starts with faith, we get a different picture. God does not have to arrive at the conclusion to a deductive argument or inductive investigation of nature, but instead God is there at the beginning, as the presupposition and premise. Believing does not have to rest on scientific evidence, any more than loving, laughing, and singing do.

If we want to teach youth science, not scientism, then we can affirm that science is not the only source of knowledge, nor always the best source. The clearest depictions we have of God—God is love, God is light, God is the creator of life—suggest we are in the realm of direct knowledge. Life, light, and love can be known directly. The person who needs scientific evidence to believe that he or she is alive is already in trouble. Likewise, parents do not need science to tell them to love their children, nor do children need it to feel the sun's light warmly on their faces. Science describes the properties of light, but the starting facts—that there is light, that we are alive, that we do love—can be known directly. We can start with God.

Starting with science squeezes out faith, but starting with faith leaves ample room for science. Just as the framework of Christ's divinity accommodates his humanity and expands human potential, so too the framework of faith accommodates science and can even expand our scientific sensibility. It is worth mentioning two ways faith has aided science.

First, science has grown remarkably well in cultures influenced by Judeo-Christian faith. Certainly, science can grow in other cultures too, but there are good theological reasons why Judaism and Christianity provided receptive soil for science. Human existence is unpredictable, and so too were the deities of most ancient cultures. Humans were seen as pawns in the gods' rage-filled battles with other gods. Gloucester in *King Lear* depicts this sense of divine caprice: "As flies to wanton schoolboys are we to the gods; they kill us for their sport."

But not so for the children of Abraham and Sarah. Their hope was built on God's reliable *hesed*—God's steadfast loving-kindness. Not only God's love, but also God's laws were declared to be constant, predictable, and even universal. As Hadley Arkes has noted, the Ten Commandments were not a set of municipal regulations intended to govern the vicinity around Mount Sinai; rather, their jurisdiction was universal. It gives a different cast to life when people perceive it has a God-given universal order. It inspires the scientific drive to discover constant laws in nature. By contrast, it saps the scientific impulse if reality is viewed as being capricious and chaotic.

Though scientists may not all believe in God, they do all have faith in an orderly universe. Einstein reportedly remarked that the most incomprehensible thing about the universe is the fact that it *is* comprehensible. We can make sense of it. Scientists approach their work with a sense that everything has a hidden order beneath the surface, waiting to be discovered. The chemist and philosopher Michael Polanyi described how scientists are all people of faith in the sense that they maintain a passionate trust in the order and intelligibility of the physical universe.[1]

In speaking of passion, Polanyi brings us to a second way that the framework of faith can expand our understanding of science. Science not only inherits the premise that the universe is orderly; it also, like Christian faith, has a passionate, personal dimension.

Though one might suppose the scientific stance is cold, detached, and "objective," Polanyi explains how the personal and relational aspects of science are crucial for making discoveries. Scientists bring to their investigation any number of personal judgments, hunches, and intuitions as well as the tacit embodiment of a scientific tradition. There is an I-Thou relationality in faith that summons personal commitment, and also an I-object relationality in science that likewise calls for personal commitment. In both faith and science, we see the human desire to indwell, the longing to know inwardly and intimately.

Much more could be said about the nature of faith and science, but let's turn our attention now to the process of teaching youth—in particular, teaching them about the one issue that has caused more trouble than any other: creation and evolution.

Thus far, we have diagnosed problems, such as scientism and fideism, that can occur when science and faith interact and have proposed principles and guidelines toward a solution to these conflicts. We have

[1] Michael Polanyi, *Personal Knowledge: Toward a Post-critical Philosophy* (Chicago: University of Chicago Press, 2015).

discussed how the more severe problem is not conflict but instead non-interaction, hence the struggle of young people to live in parallel universes: the Sunday world of faith, the Monday world of science and technology. In response, we have proposed a universe-based approach to youth ministry that begins with the description of Jesus as one Person in two natures. This pattern gives us a model for relating faith and science in a way that honors their different natures yet also unifies them into one reality. In the process of relating, we become attuned to how faith and science can complement and even correct each other. Science can correct the exaggerating tendency of faith, while faith corrects the reducing tendency of science.

Let's now put this process into practice by looking at evolution, which is so frequently the elephant in the room during discussions of faith and science with young people. How did the elephant get into the room in the first place? Did it lumber off the ark or climb inch by inch out of some prebiotic ooze? This question points to conflict, but the conflict in turn can be a gift. It means faith and science are being summoned to interact, and this interaction—though it is often, at present, a negative one—can lead us to new and positive insights.

PART II

CREATION AND EVOLUTION

CHAPTER 15

A Curious and Sensitive Lad

As a boy, Charles Darwin had a large appetite for nature. Hunting for beetles in some dead bark one day, he spotted a rare kind, which he cupped and held in his hand. Another rare beetle appeared. He scooped it up with the other hand. Next, he recounts, I saw "a third and new kind, which I could not bear to lose, so that I popped the one which I held in my right hand into my mouth. Alas, it ejected some intensely acrid fluid, which burnt my tongue so that I was forced to spit the beetle." In the process, his fingers unfolded, allowing a second beetle to escape.[1]

The beetle escaped the grip of his hand but not his mind. In time, his fascination turned from beetles to barnacles, then to various other forms of life, and ultimately to the question of how these "endless forms most beautiful and most wonderful have been evolved."[2] This quotation is the final sentence of the *Origin of Species* and the only place in the first edition of the book where he actually uses the word *evolved*. But the word gained traction among scientists, and there is no doubt that credit for the modern theory of biological evolution should go to Charles Darwin, along with Alfred Russel Wallace.

[1] David Quammen, *The Reluctant Mr. Darwin: An Intimate Portrait of Charles Darwin and the Making of His Theory of Evolution* (New York: W. W. Norton, 2006), 244.
[2] Charles Darwin, *On the Origin of Species: A Facsimile of the First Edition* (Cambridge, MA: Harvard University Press, 2001), 490.

Darwin has thus been cast as both superhero and villain, yet looking at his growing-up years and beyond, we see a more ordinary and sympathetic character: an English schoolboy engrossed in the observation of nature, of the same species as Wordsworth, Constable, Dawkins, and the Oundle School chaplain. In his teenage years and into his twenties, Darwin held orthodox Christian beliefs, and he seems to have held them earnestly. During the five-year explorations of the *Beagle*, the crew teased young Charles for his tendency to quote the Bible.[3] Prior to that naturalist voyage and well before he became the world's most famous scientist, Darwin went to Cambridge University with the idea of becoming a clergyman.

He may have seen Anglican ordination as a way to pursue his naturalist interests. The nineteenth-century English parson could lead a quiet country life, with enough free time to study God's creation. Though he did not keep to this trajectory, Darwin exemplifies the historic connection between church vocation and scientific avocation. He also exemplifies the struggle of young people to see life through the eyes of both science and faith. The rocks upon which his faith floundered are still in the water today.

Since Charles Darwin's struggles were not unique, it is worth considering what happened to his faith and whether things might have gone differently for him. Clearly, his wife, Emma, had prayed they would. She cried over his losing Christian faith, and he in turn cried over her tears. But Charles Darwin faced stiff obstacles. Some were intellectual, and some were emotional. Some were scientific, some theological. But none, it could be argued, were as implacable as they might have appeared.

Let us imagine we are doing ministry with a young Charles Darwin. Our goal is simple: we want the Bible-quoting boy to go on to become a lifelong disciple of Jesus Christ. Even if the boy still decides to become a full-time scientist and not an Anglican priest, the goal of mature Christian faith still pertains.

Doing ministry with a young Charles Darwin does not require that we earn a degree in biology. Instead, we can focus primarily on three time-honored activities of ministry: praying, reading the Bible, and doing

---

[3] Quammen, *The Reluctant Mr. Darwin*, 245.

theology with him. Science will enter into our ministry because it is an interest of his and because it is part of the cultural waters in which we swim. Bringing the gospel to our present-day culture entails having at least some scientific literacy. But we don't all need to be science teachers. As Charles shares what he is learning, our educational ministry can consist mainly in prayer, Bible reading, and theology.

Here are three proposed guidelines. First, in prayer, we ask the Holy Spirit to be our Teacher. Jesus promises in John's Gospel that the Holy Spirit "will teach you everything" (14:26), and in prayer we take him up on this promise. Second, in Bible reading, we pay attention to the theology that arises from our interpretations of Scripture. Third, in doing theology, we pay attention to the emotions that arise from our theological doctrines.

With these guidelines in mind, we can look at some problems Darwin faced. Two pressing intellectual problems were immutability and the *imago Dei*. Two recurring emotional problems were the suffering that suffuses the struggle for existence and the seeming futility of this struggle—its end in death. Intellect and emotions swirl together here, as everywhere in youth ministry, but let's try to analyze these problems one by one.

First, immutability. Immutable means unchanging—not evolving. Theologians and naturalists alike held that God is immutable, and so too are created species. The reliability of the natural world had fueled science in the first place; it meant that there were natural "laws" and other sorts of order waiting to be discovered. God created living things "according to their kinds" (Gen 1:11, 12, 21, 24, and 25). One kind, therefore, could not turn into another. Darwin's mind said otherwise. He was drawn toward the idea of "transmutation," which said that one species could and did turn into another. He proposed that this process was gradual. It happened by infinitesimal increments, over long stretches of time.

Darwin did not invent the idea of transmutation. It had been in the air for some time and was first articulated in 1800 by French naturalist Jean-Baptiste Lamarck, whom some historians would call the grandfather of evolution. But Darwin was the first to take hold of transmutation and develop it into the full-blown theory of evolution by identifying the mechanisms that caused organisms to undergo continual change.

Transmutation, as he saw it, needed no divine intervention but instead three all-natural ingredients: random variation, natural selection, and vast periods of time. In a given population of species, some members are going to be randomly different (random variation), and some differences are going to prove advantageous for survival, procreation, and increased population (natural selection); and over the long haul (vast periods of time), the divergent and flourishing new population within the species will diverge so much that it can no longer procreate with the old population. At this point, the two populations are considered distinct species.

This idea of transmutation hit Darwin with emotional force. Did it damage his faith? It may have done so. David Quammen suggests it damaged his health. His work in this area of transmutation coincided with complaints of mysterious ailments—"jumpy heart, nausea, vomiting, headaches, nervous excitement, inordinate flatulence."[4] Regardless of any connections between transmutation, loss of faith, and increase of flatulence, let's sort out what we can. Imagine you are doing ministry with a young Charles Darwin. The question is whether a long, natural process of producing endless varieties of species runs counter to a plain reading of Genesis in which God produced a fixed number of "kinds" through immediate, special acts of creation.

It would appear the two narratives are in direct conflict. If *bara'* or "create" in Genesis means bringing molecules, cells, plants, animals, and so forth into physical existence, then a plain reading of Genesis suggests that God did this work in the span of six days, and various species arrived on the scene fully formed. Conflict seems inescapable, unless one could somehow make the case that *bara'* in Genesis does *not* mean bringing physical matter into existence—unless, that is, "create" does not entail configuring organisms into their physical form. This is precisely the question we will take up a bit later, though we must admit that the idea of a creation that is not physically focused sounds very odd to people living in an age of science.

---

[4] Quammen, *The Reluctant Mr. Darwin*, 37.

A second problem for Darwin was the *imago Dei*, or image of God. Growing up, young Charles had learned that people are different from all other species, having been specially made in God's image. Gradually his mind began to waver. Transmutation led him inevitably to the idea that all species share a common ancestry. Later life-forms point back to earlier life forms, and altogether they point to a time, many eons ago, when a few life-forms, or even just one, started to give rise to the multitude.

Darwin struggled with this idea of common ancestry because people appear to be so different from animals. Species *other* than humans could share a common origin. "But Man—wonderful Man," Darwin writes in his journal, "is an exception." Humanity must be an exception to this rule of common origins because people are created in God's image. And yet, Darwin reasons further, a human being is clearly a mammal. Three lines after writing his first statement about humanity, Darwin changes his mind and declares the opposite: "He is no exception."[5]

The idea that all species are interrelated has a certain elegance. But by drawing humans closer to all forms of life, from apes to amoebas, common ancestry threatened to draw "wonderful Man" apart from his special relationship with God. The doctrine of *imago Dei*, as it was articulated in Darwin's day, spoke of human distinction from, not relatedness to, other life-forms. Common ancestry was the second rock upon which Darwin's faith floundered, and it must have felt larger and sharper than the first.

A way to rethink this problem has already been suggested. Common physical origins need not impede faith, provided we maintain a lively sense of God's transforming power. If God can transform water into wine, or wine into blood, then humanity's starting point in history sets no limitation upon our God-given destiny. However, at issue here is not just what God is able to do but what God in fact decided to do. The problem is not making theological sense of common ancestry but finding biblical warrant to do so. The same people who had read Genesis and saw immutability of species also saw God's special creation of humanity from the dust of the earth.

---

[5] Quammen, *The Reluctant Mr. Darwin*, 37.

Though once a Bible-quoting boy, Darwin could not reconcile his scientific idea of common ancestry with any theological interpretation of Genesis he had been taught. Embracing common ancestry meant turning his back on Scripture. He did not, however, totally divest his theory of divine power. In a later edition of *Origin of Species*, he identified "the Creator" as the One who breathed life into the first life-forms. Some readers suspect Darwin was bowing to pressure from a Christian public or from his publisher or was perhaps hoping to calm his wife. Whatever his reasons, he was not alone. Scientists of his century were much more apt to include God in their scientific writings. But even if a Creator or Prime Mover had started the whole process of evolution, Darwin also decided there was no ongoing divine involvement: there was no intentional design, nor did any loving hand direct the outcomes. Darwin perceived a completely impersonal process. It might have sounded cold, yet he developed a warm attachment to his theory, and he called it his "child."

From the start, his child was vulnerable to attack from scientists who said that material causes alone could not explain all the stunning complexity we find in nature. So much of it looks to be designed. If you see a smart phone lying on the beach, you don't think random physical events in the ocean washed it ashore. Rather, you infer a designing mind behind the specimen. The argument in Darwin's day involved pocket watches and eyeballs, but the basic point was the same: the degree of natural complexity points to a supernatural designing Mind. Many of Darwin's colleagues simply could not believe the evolutionary process was solely physical.

Alfred Russel Wallace was in this latter camp. He claimed natural evolution alone could not account for the human brain. Instead, said Wallace, an "Overruling Intelligence" had directed such a marvelous outcome. Wallace was the man who some years earlier had formulated the basic ideas of evolution independently from Darwin. He was about to publish his discoveries before Darwin could finish his opus. But Darwin had influential friends in the scientific community who stepped in and arranged for the two men to receive joint credit for the theory. Now, however, Wallace was about to publish another article, proposing that an Overruling

Intelligence guided the evolutionary development of the human brain. When he got wind of it, Darwin was not pleased. He wrote to Wallace, "I hope you have not murdered too completely your own & my child."[6]

The human brain at the end of the process was the issue for Wallace. Today, the first cell at the start of the process appears equally baffling. The cell turned out to be infinitely more complex than nineteenth-century scientists had anticipated. It is harder to evolve chemicals into a cell than to evolve a single cell into a person.[7] Scientists recognize this problem and are working on it. Telling biologists that an organic process is too complex is like telling an alpine climber a mountain is too steep. Scientists are committed to explaining all life-forms in terms of physical cause and effect. And Darwin's theory became the harbinger of this completely modern approach.

Transmutation and common ancestry were intellectual threats to the Christian worldview of young Darwin. But they were not the biggest obstacles to his faith. Those two scientific difficulties probably paled in comparison with theological problems he faced. Specifically, Darwin could not square belief in a loving God with the suffering and death that permeate life on earth. In his scientific research, he observed endless suffering in the animal world. In his personal life, he experienced suffering and death firsthand. Suffering and death were no doubt the biggest rocks to shipwreck his faith.

---

[6] Quammen, *The Reluctant Mr. Darwin*, 216.
[7] H. Allen Orr, "Darwin vs. Intelligent Design (Again)," *Boston Review* 21, 1996–97, cited in Karl Giberson, *Species of Origins: America's Search for a Creation Story* (Lanham, MD: Rowman & Littlefield, 2002), 27. "Harder" is, of course, an anthropomorphic way of describing the impersonal evolutionary process.

CHAPTER 16

Cruel Suffering

Darwin's older brother was a doctor. At age sixteen, Charles also embarked on a course of medical training but soon gave it up. Doctors in those days routinely performed operations without anesthetic. The horrific pain of these procedures revolted him.[1]

By all accounts, Darwin had a tender heart. Once, as a boy, he was cruel to a puppy. He carried feelings of guilt about it sixty years later.[2]

He could picture the suffering of people or puppies and of lesser creatures too. In later life, he was still interested in beetles. W. D. Crick (grandfather of Francis Crick, one of the people who discovered DNA) sent him a large beetle to examine. The beetle was mailed through the postal service and arrived in poor shape.

Darwin wrote back to Crick, "As the wretched beetle was still feebly alive, I have put it in a bottle with chopped laurel leaves, that it may die an easy and quicker death."[3] That Darwin would think to practice euthanasia on a beetle tells us something about his sensitivity.

John Calvin called faith "a firm and certain knowledge of God's benevolence toward us."[4] This was precisely the kind of faith that Darwin

[1] Quammen, *The Reluctant Mr. Darwin*, 33.
[2] Quammen, *The Reluctant Mr. Darwin*, 244.
[3] Quammen, *The Reluctant Mr. Darwin*, 253.
[4] John Calvin, *Institutes of the Christian Religion*, ed. John T. McNeil, trans. Ford Lewis Battles (Philadelphia: Westminster, 1960), 551.

lacked. Looking at nature, he did not see benevolence. Cats torture mice. Ichneumon wasps lay their eggs inside living caterpillars, and when the eggs hatch, the larvae eat the caterpillar from the inside out. Why would a benevolent God design such a process? This was a question Darwin had, and it was clearly a why question of faith, not a scientific how question. He knew well enough how the process worked.

His friend Asa Gray at Harvard University was both a biologist and a Christian believer. Darwin told Gray, "I cannot see, as plainly as others do, evidence of design and benevolence on all sides of us."[5]

Hardest of all to reconcile with the idea of a benevolent Ruler were the suffering and death of people closest to him. He wrote again to Gray, several months later, "An innocent & good man stands under [a] tree & is killed by [a] flash of lightening. Do you believe (& I really shd like to hear) that God *designedly* killed this man? Many or most persons do believe this; I can't & don't."[6]

This letter feels closest to the core of his disbelief. The person Darwin must have had in mind was not a hypothetical man standing under a hypothetical tree. It was his daughter, Annie, who had recently died a painful death, probably of tuberculosis, at age ten. His father had died three years earlier. Sometime between the two deaths, Darwin said he "gave up Christianity." He reported in his autobiography, "Disbelief crept over me at a very slow rate, but was at last complete."[7]

When some people lose faith, they mourn its loss, wishing they could still believe. This was not the case with Darwin. After he renounced Christian faith, his heart became settled. For he was disturbed not only by the suffering he saw in this life but equally by Christian teaching about suffering in the next. He wrote, "I can indeed hardly see how anyone ought to wish Christianity to be true; for if so the plain language of the text seems to show that the men who do not believe, and this would include

[5] Quammen, *The Reluctant Mr. Darwin*, 120.
[6] Quammen, *The Reluctant Mr. Darwin*, 120.
[7] Quammen, *The Reluctant Mr. Darwin*, 118.

my Father, Brother, and almost all my best friends, will be everlastingly punished. And this is a damnable doctrine."[8]

Hell is not a scientific issue; it has no connection to transmutation or common ancestry of species. It seems clear that Darwin's loss of faith concerned theology as much as science. Scientifically, he saw suffering across all life-forms in their struggle to survive in this world. Theologically, he was told that many humans would suffer eternally in the next. His response was not to throw himself on God's mercy, as a preacher like Jonathan Edwards or George Whitfield might have hoped. It was rather to reject the religion that espoused this teaching.

We do well to ponder Darwin's plight, for he is not alone. Though preaching on hell has long been considered an effective way to bring adolescents to conversion, there will always be sensitive souls whose meditation on everlasting torment turns their minds in the other direction.

For young Charles, the problem of suffering was conjoined to the problem of death. His mother died when he was eight years old. He could remember little about her, except her deathbed and a black velvet gown. When his father died in later life, Darwin missed the funeral. When his daughter Annie died, he again missed the funeral. When his close friend Charles Lyell died, he missed the funeral. Missing funerals was a lifelong pattern, and the reason cannot be that he did not care about these people or that he was taking a stand against the church. Funerals are typically occasions when people come closest to facing the fact of death. It seems likely that the avoidance of funerals was an avoidance of this fact. Far from not caring, Darwin may have empathized to the extreme. Funerals may have felt, even unconsciously, too close to his own burial or that of his mother.

His response to suffering and death shaped how the eyes of his heart developed and also colored his thinking as a scientist. Most scientists of his day looked at nature and saw providential design, but Darwin saw wanton cruelty. He could not imagine a benevolent, omnipotent God permitting such pain in this world and the next. If there were a god, it would

---

[8] Quammen, *The Reluctant Mr. Darwin*, 245–46.

have to be some impersonal being, similar to Aristotle's First Cause or Prime Mover. On the question of whether such a god exists, Darwin said he "must be content to remain an Agnostic."[9]

But would it have been possible for Darwin to remain a Christian—and not only to remain the kind of Christian he once was but to grow into a deeper, fuller faith that somehow takes into account the suffering and death of which he had become so acutely aware? Amid suffering and death, could he have seen, through eyes of the heart, an infinitely loving God revealed to him in Jesus Christ? For many young people today, as for young Charles, the problems of faith are scientific, theological, emotional, and spiritual, all swirled together. The solution involves seeing through both the eyes of science and eyes of the heart, distinctly but also together.

Stories of suffering are personal, and they summon a pastoral response. But theological discussion also has its time and place, and as a starting point, we could note that all origin narratives are replete with painful cataclysm. Maybe there is an exception somewhere—some tropical island where everyone lives disease-free lives and then dies peacefully in their sleep, so the elders tell their offspring about an earth that began in a painless birth. But for the bulk of humanity and sweep of history, suffering and death are ever-looming facts of life. In Genesis, a world of humans and animals drown in a flood of pounding rain that will not stop. In evolution, humans emerge from eons of warfare that pits the desperation of avoiding being eaten against the desperation of avoiding starvation.

More recently, some biologists have suggested that nature is really not so "red in tooth and claw" as Tennyson supposed. Noting that cooperation is vital to the survival of most species, some have recast the evolutionary "struggle for existence" as being more accurately a "*snuggle* for existence."[10] This new focus on cooperation, symbiosis, and community has obvious merit. At the same time, certain facts of the food chain seem inescapable. I have lain awake at night, in a bed in Kenya, listening to a pack of hyenas *cooperate* in killing what must have been a very large

---

[9] Quammen, *The Reluctant Mr. Darwin*, 246.
[10] Martin Nowak, *SuperCooperators: Altruism, Evolution, and Why We Need Each Other to Succeed* (New York: Simon and Schuster, 2011).

creature. The process was long and loud. Perhaps, like Darwin, I am overly sensitive, but I can still hear the high-pitched whoops of the hyenas and agonizing bellows of their prey.

We can accept a degree of suffering if it serves a good purpose—training for a big game or studying for an exam are examples of sensible suffering—but so much suffering seems pointless, and the duration of pointless suffering in evolution is mind-blowing. Reintroduce God into the framework of evolution, and it seems to be a recipe for cynicism. For two hundred thousand years or more, *Homo sapiens* are on the scene. What was God doing before appearing to Abraham just four thousand years ago? Was God standing back and smiling as successive generations of people got eaten by animals or died from rotten teeth? Atheists delight in taunting believers with these sorts of questions.

The comment about dying from bad teeth was a ubiquitous debating point for the English atheist Christopher Hitchens. Hitchens serves as a more recent example of the dynamic we just observed with Darwin: though intellectual reasons are given for loss of faith, the back story frequently discloses some intensely personal emotional roots.

Hitchens argues that belief in God is actually morally wrong[11] because *"religion poisons everything."*[12] Religion's toxicity is his constant refrain, which appears like a Greek chorus throughout his book *God Is Not Great: How Religion Poisons Everything.* All his case studies from world history point in the same neon-lit direction to the same inevitable conclusion: religion kills; it *"poisons everything"* (italics his, repeatedly).[13] He claims this poisoning effect is universal, applying to all religions, all believers, everywhere. But when we turn to his autobiographical writings, we hear concern for one believer in particular—his mother.

Hitchens describes his affection for his mother, who taught him a love of books and who was overall the bright spot in his childhood. He also recalls the day his mother announced she was leaving his father to live

---

[11] Christopher Hitchens, *God Is Not Great: How Religion Poisons Everything* (New York: Hachette, 2007), 103.
[12] Hitchens, *God Is Not Great*, 13.
[13] Hitchens, *God Is Not Great*, 25.

with an ex–Anglican priest. Mother and priest had both become "devotees of the Maharishi Mahesh Yogi: the sinister windbag who had brought enlightenment to the Beatles in the summer of love."[14] Some months later, he found out their explorations had taken them to Athens, where they both died in a hotel room, in a pact of suicide. His mother died by poisoning—a toxic overdose of sleeping pills.[15]

In general, when young people come with intellectual doubts and questions about faith, we do well to listen for some question behind their question, which is often emotional and personal. Emotional issues often lurk behind intellectual doubts. This point needs to be stressed, though not stressed so much that we fall into the opposite error.

The opposite error would be to focus only on feelings, avoiding scientific or theological questions because we feel incompetent to discuss them. Intellectual questions also require intellectual answers. At the start of a junior high retreat, I asked whether there were any preliminary questions. I anticipated answering queries about the location of the bathrooms or soda machine. Right away, a hand shot up. Looking down at notes he had brought with him, an eighth-grade boy asked, "How can God be both three and one, because that sounds mathematically impossible?" And nearly in the same breath, "How can Jesus be both human and divine, because God is infinite, and humans are not?"

Many youth ministers would prefer to talk about a teenager's love life than deal with such questions, though it is such questions that lead to deeper faith. Even if we cannot plumb the depths of theology and science, we can grow in these areas. It is not enough to tell youth we admire their courage in asking tough questions; we need also to have our own courage to answer them. Our answers may not be final or perfect, but they can at least be good enough to enable youth to have higher-quality doubts and questions. We can tell youth what we know and acknowledge we are still learning. We can tell them at times that we simply don't know something,

---

[14] Christopher Hitchens, *Hitch-22: A Memoir* (New York: Hachette, 2010), 19.
[15] Hitchens, *Hitch-22*, 24.

and hopefully this response will come from humility and not laziness. Here theology can take a page from science: when scientists do not know something, they often look for ways to find out.

Before I speak more fully to the issues of creation and evolution just raised, let me make two general comments regarding conflicts between faith and science. First, these conflicts can be good and certainly better than non-interaction. Discovery often starts with conflict. Something doesn't fit or make sense, and we struggle to figure out why. Two travelers on the road to Emmaus (Luke 24) feel the rending conflict between their fervent hope that Jesus would be their Messiah and the dreadful fact of his crucifixion. Working through this conflict leads them to a new vision of Jesus, in the breaking of the bread, and it leads to a new view of salvation. Likewise, when young people work through conflicts involving science, the effort can bring them, too, to deeper vision.

Second, when dealing with these conflicts, it's good to remember a basic fact about the human brain. The intellect of the brain is connected to the emotions. Powerful ideas can stir us emotionally. For scientists and believers alike, big discoveries may bring tears to the eyes. By the same token, powerful emotions are bound to shape our thinking. Intellectual doubts sometimes have strong emotional components. Behind a question of theodicy—of why, if God is all-powerful, the world has so much pain and evil—there is often a poignant personal story waiting to be heard. Whether a conflict is emotional, intellectual, or both, it can have layers. A psychologist used to say that couples never argue about money. Of course, on the surface, some couples are constantly bickering about credit cards and bank balances. But underneath, the arguments involve issues of power, trust, and control.

In this vein, Darwin's loss of faith was not just a problem of science. It involved acute personal losses: his mother when he was eight, his daughter when she was ten. These sources of disbelief may have run deeper than any intellectual doubts prompted by evolution. Or to shift the focus somewhat, behind today's efforts to oppose evolution and rebuild the "foundations of Genesis," we can often hear despondency about the social and moral revolutions of the past sixty years—a different kind of loss, to be sure, but still worth acknowledging.

Having said all that, what now can we say to young Charles or to some actual youth you happen to know who invokes science as the reason their faith is shrinking at the same time their intellect is growing?

CHAPTER 17

Exploring Options

One option for teaching youth would be a "science says" approach. Here we would prepare young people to update or discard theological doctrines on the basis of new scientific evidence. After all, the idea of immutability is just an idea; it is not God. If science dictates transmutation, then discard immutability. If science shows common ancestry, then dismiss the idea of the *imago Dei*, or else rework it to fit the new framework.

A science-says approach appears to make sense to many people. Since Darwin's day, human exceptionalism has lost ground, and transmutation has gained considerable traction, so much so that the idea of evolution is now applied even to God. Liberal process theologians and evangelical "open theists" both propose that God is also undergoing continual change and growth. We can discuss the merits of their proposals another day, but suffice it to say that a science-says approach means we must be ready and willing to change our theology on an ongoing basis.

I hope it is not simply resistance to change that makes me reject a science-says approach but rather the desire to have a right relationship between faith and science. Modern science can never detect divine action. As the preceding pages have stressed, science investigates powerfully and exclusively the material dimensions of reality. A science-says approach starts out promising a God who is bigger—big enough to transcend all our previous theological constructs. But in the end, it delivers a God small enough to fit within the confines of scientific paradigms. If we revise our faith solely on the grounds of scientific evidence, we will lose first the loaves and fishes, then the resurrection, then ultimately the existence of the God to whom we pray. We want science but not science alone.

To be sure, science can beneficially prompt us to revisit our theology. Regarding the *imago Dei*, we can teach youth that it is not meant to be a biological description but a statement of God's relationship with humanity. Regarding immutability, we can say that when God created vegetation, sea monsters, winged birds, and wild animals according to their kinds, these words show God appreciates both order and variety; they do not outlaw transmutation. Given these revised readings, the sharp rocks of immutability and the *imago Dei* become smoother stones, possibly stepping-stones to deeper faith. But a science-says approach cannot get us there. The moment we speak of God, we are pushing past what science says.

An opposite option for teaching youth would be a "Bible says" approach. Since the Bible offers timeless truth, a Bible-says approach would mean we teach youth to reject any claims of science that run counter to the Bible or, more accurately, counter to our current reading of the Bible. If our Bible reading tells us neo-Darwinian evolution did not happen, then youth ministers following a Bible-says approach would teach young people to reject outright the idea that it did. After all, does the theory of neo-Darwinian evolution really have any solid evidence to back it up?

Scientists are adamant it does. They point to the fossil record. Some species are always found at lower levels than other species—evidence, they say, that the higher and later evolved from the lower and earlier. Second, they point to the fact that drug companies are constantly developing new types of antibiotics to combat new strains of bacteria—evidence, they say, that evolution is still happening today. Above all, they point to DNA. When species have strikingly similar genomes, including extra and apparently useless information embedded in their genes, biologists view this fact as good evidence the different species evolved from an earlier, common ancestor.

In an age of specialization, hardly anyone has time to study and scrutinize all this evidence for themselves. We come to trust experts. If ten

DNA experts agree a paternity test proves Joe is the father of a child, Joe is going to have to pay child support even if he doesn't like the experts or the evidence. Evolution is not a paternity test, but scientists say it is similar in that both involve drawing conclusions from genetic information.

However, with a Bible-says approach, we could find our own science experts who are willing to swim against the stream. Maybe their numbers are few, but this fact can be pegged to a rigged system that brooks no opposition to neo-Darwinian evolution. Our few but eminently quotable Bible-says scientists can explain to our youth that all the evidence just mentioned admits an alternate explanation. The similar DNA means God reused good blueprints; all the "unnecessary" information will in time be revealed to have good present-day purposes. The new strains of bacteria are just that—new strains, not a whole new species or family of species. The fossil record is dubious, debatable, and has numerous gaps; just look at how evolutionists themselves argue over the Cambrian explosion. One or two references to the Cambrian explosion should be enough to convince our youth that our Bible-says experts know what they are talking about.

Evolutionary biologists do in fact engage in lively intramural debates. But they all agree that their disputes over how evolution happened should not be portrayed to the public as doubts that it did. If crime investigators debate whether a dead body is the result of a murder, suicide, or accident, all sides in the dispute have no doubt they are looking at a corpse. Most biologists see themselves in a similar position with regard to evolution.

If we are looking to foster productive dialogue between mainstream scientists and creationists, we could ask in a general way whether physical causes alone can account for all the physical evidence we see. Can DNA arise from random matter and motion? How do physical matter and energy arise in the first place? These questions are not unreasonable to ask. But the kind of Bible-says approach we are talking about goes much further. It says certain ways of reading scientific evidence are, as a foregone conclusion, going to be ruled out of bounds due to certain ways we have of reading the Bible. Since neo-Darwinian evolution has such widespread acceptance among scientists, clearly a Bible-says approach would mean our youth must be ready to hold some very unpopular views.

I hope it is not fear of unpopularity that makes me reject this kind of Bible-says approach but rather concern for a good understanding of biblical authority. The Bible is living and active. Some of the most important transformations in church history, including the Protestant Reformation and Pentecostal Revival, have been sparked by people returning to the Bible and rereading it with fresh eyes of the heart. In placing the Bible into human hands, God saw fit to give us rabbis, teachers, bishops, prophets, apostles—and preeminently, the Holy Spirit—to help us read it rightly. The best readings, it seems to me, show humility—both the humility to respect the interpretations of our forebears and the humility to receive the ongoing guidance of the Holy Spirit.

For example, the apostle Paul learned growing up that circumcision was essential to a covenant relationship with God. The circumcision rule was given to Abraham and reiterated throughout the Bible. But Paul did not take a Bible-says approach with respect to Gentile believers in Jesus. He reread the Bible and came to the conclusion that they did not need to be circumcised in order to be in right relationship with God. Their faith in Christ was sufficient.

When a Bible-says approach shuts out new illumination, it can lock us into readings that are not actually God given. In Darwin's day and long thereafter, people reading Genesis saw some things that seemed nearly as clear as the circumcision rule. It seemed obvious, for example, that *bara'* (ברא), or "create," meant to bring into physical existence. Also that *min* (מין), or "kinds," meant what modern biologists were calling species. And so, when God created living things according to their kinds, it meant that species were brought into physical existence in their finished form, thus ruling out the possibility that "endless forms most beautiful and most wonderful"[1] could ever have evolved.

Faithful Christians may not feel compelled to revisit any aspect of this reading of Genesis. But the Bible-says approach just outlined goes further; it says they are forbidden to do so. This approach starts out promising a Bible that is big—big enough to cover every area and facet of life. But in

[1] Darwin, *On the Origin of Species*, 490.

the end, it delivers a Bible that is smaller—small enough to fit within the confines of prior interpretations, now hardened into doctrine. I am not about to treat doctrine lightly; it is a part of youth education that I hold in high regard. But I hold the Bible in still higher esteem, and the Holy Spirit highest of all. Accordingly, we first pray, then read, then form doctrines. And here, "we" means the whole church, around the world and down through the ages. Rejecting the kind of Bible-says approach just outlined implies not an overall skepticism of the Bible but only skepticism of the person who says, "This is what the Bible means, once and for all."

In conclusion, a science-says approach and a Bible-says approach both suffer from a similar shortcoming. In different ways, they both block the revelation of God's Spirit and hinder the eyes of the heart from opening more widely. The science-says approach does it by screening out the spiritual dimension; the Bible-says approach by fitting the spiritual dimension into a fixed box.

Is there a third approach to teaching young people that avoids these pitfalls? I think there is. We could call it the "It seemed good to the Holy Spirit and to us" approach. Admittedly, this phrase is a mouthful. But let's describe the approach first before searching for a better name.

CHAPTER 18

"It Seemed Good to the Holy Spirit and to Us"

I n Acts, the apostles at first assumed new believers in Jesus would need to follow all the rules that God gave to their Jewish ancestors. It made sense. They were Jewish. Jesus was Jewish. To follow Jesus, you needed to be Jewish, which for boys or men meant, first and foremost, you needed to be circumcised.

Then new evidence started coming in. Peter reported that uncircumcised Gentiles were receiving the Holy Spirit, just as the apostles had on Pentecost. They were even speaking in tongues, just as the apostles had.

The apostles held a council in Jerusalem, and there they reached a verdict on what requirements of the old covenant should remain in force under the new. They delivered their decision to the churches, framing it this way: "It seemed good to the Holy Spirit and to us" (Acts 15:28). Using their powers of reason, they allowed the Holy Spirit to guide their thinking. New evidence propelled them to reread Scriptures and re-form doctrine. The process was clearly communal and probably intensely prayerful.

Scientific evidence today is not the same as church evidence back then, but science can also propel us to ask again and to see anew what God is revealing. When it comes to issues of evolution and creation, or anything else, we hope to arrive at the place where we can say to young people, "It seemed good to the Holy Spirit and to us."

The goal, therefore, is to offer something more than just our private opinions—namely, a reading that flows from the Spirit's guidance and that catches the sense of believers around the world and across time. In keeping with the Chalcedonian pattern, we let science speak in its language, using its rules and its evidence. We also let faith speak, using rules and evidence that are internal to the church. In this way, faith and science can illuminate and correct each other.

On some questions, science is very clear, on others murky, and on some silent, but always a scientific sensibility serves to check an exaggerating tendency of faith. Meanwhile, faith is always working to correct the reducing tendency of science. This Spirit-focused approach is not science says or Bible says but a relationality of faith and science. The Holy Spirit has been called the "go-between God," an informal description that depicts the inherent relationality of the Holy Trinity. God's love is always seeking to go between, intercede, mediate, and reconcile. Here we are asking the Spirit to help us reconcile the insights of faith and science.

The following pages will offer a proposal for reconciling faith and science with regard to issues of creation and evolution. This territory has been well plowed, and some readers may have creation-and-evolution fatigue. But hopefully new insights can spark fresh interest.

A couple of reminders. First, the pattern of Chalcedon means science and faith need to be kept distinct. We are not going to ask biology to rule on the Bible. Genesis speaks of God's activity, which modern science is not designed to detect. Likewise, we are not going to ask Genesis to turn itself into a science textbook. The Bible contains no graphs, formulas, or equations, even though God knows all the science in the world and then some. However, revealing modern science to ancient people was evidently not God's top priority.

Second, the pattern of Chalcedon means science and faith need to become unified into one vision of reality. Their distinct insights need to cohere and not contradict. Otherwise youth will be pulled in two directions and most likely opt for the road best traveled—a material worldview marked out by science and technology. So the goal is a *union without confusion* of faith and science. "Without confusion" means not mixing together their different ways of knowing.

This goal can be hard to attain because confusion can creep in unawares. We are dealing with entire ways of reading reality, yet we don't always stop to remove and examine the theoretical glasses that shape our vision; and indeed we cannot do so without employing some other theoretical lens. Living in an age of science, we see reality in physical terms. We see this way even when reading the Bible, though we know the Bible is focused preeminently on spiritual realities.

For instance, corporations and churches alike will talk about their "DNA." Clearly corporate DNA is an image for something nonphysical, but it is an image that shows how our minds work. We automatically head in the physical direction. What does it mean to be alive? You are alive if you have a beating heart and functioning brain. What is human existence? Existence means having a physical body with material molecules. But those answers come from modern science, not the Bible. In the Bible, the physical is real but often recedes to the background, while relational and spiritual dimensions move to the fore.

To read the Bible aright, we need to think in its terms, not the terms of modern science. As a prime example, the Gospel of John describes Jesus by saying, "In him was life" (John 1:4). Here "life" does not mean "In him was thirty-three years of biological existence." That statement would be accurate but wholly inadequate. "In him was life" means much more than a beating heart and electric brain. Life here means that every impulse, every breath in Jesus consists in love for God and thus love for humanity. *In him was life*—every thought, every action is done out of obedience to God, and therefore out of a desire to save people and liberate them from bondage to sin and death (Heb 2:14).

And what is death? Death is more than a flat line on the heart monitor. Death is first and foremost a spiritual condition that can affect people who are busily at work or actively engaged in recreation. A person walking down the street can still be "dead through trespasses and sins" (Eph 2:1). And by the same token, a person lying in the grave can still be alive in Christ. Life and death have dimensions beyond the physical; they have spiritual, relational dimensions more vital than material molecules.

Most Christians can grasp this idea. Most can perceive that "life" in Jesus does not mean solely or even primarily biological existence. But do we allow this idea to seep back into our reading of Genesis?

Usually not. Instead of reading the creation of Adam and Eve as a window into the spiritual realities of life and death, it seems easier, more "natural," and more "plain" to read creation in Genesis as an account of how the first *Homo sapiens* came on the scene. But we need to go back and revisit. Is creation in Genesis really talking about God configuring the first material molecules into their first physical form? When God begins to create, a physical earth already exists, along with physical water (Gen 1:2). This fact is often overlooked, yet it should prompt us to reconsider what it means for God to create and for people to be created.

The Hebrew word for "create" is *bara'*. This word is used about fifty times in the Old Testament, and always it refers to God. Only God creates; only God does *bara'*. People can make a lot of stuff, but *bara'* does not necessarily entail making something physical. Some Bible language experts would argue that nowhere in the Old Testament does *bara'* require a material meaning. Expert or not, we can all see places where creating (*bara'*) is clearly *not* a physical operation. When David prays, "*Create* in me a clean heart, O God" (Ps 51:10), he is not asking God for an angioplasty. Physical molecules are not the point.

Likewise, Isaiah uses *bara'* to speak of God *creating* Israel (Isa 43:1) and of God *creating* Jerusalem (65:18). Isaiah is not referring to a physical building project but rather to God redeeming and restoring people. If creating is not physical in these verses, then what about Genesis? What could God be doing in Genesis if not causing molecules to spring into existence?

God is doing relational creation. God is speaking to the earth and making it God's own—God's home. God is ordering the universe, separating one thing from another, giving things their identity in relation to God and thus their true "life." God is appointing, ordaining, and anointing the physical universe to have purpose. God is setting all things—including vegetation, living creatures, and people in particular—into right relationship with God and therefore right relationship with each other.

The phrase *relational creation* may sound like a new contemporary term, but it points to an ancient understanding. The modern mind says existence consists in physical substance. I am alive because I have a functioning brain that produces ideas and emotions. The modern mind thinks this way, but the ancient people whom God employed to write the Bible did not. For one thing, they probably supposed ideas and emotions came from the heart and kidneys, but more importantly, they did not think an assortment of physical organs could add up to existence. To exist, a thing or person needed to have meaning, function, order, and purpose. To exist, you needed to have a name.

In the desert, Moses wants to know God's name. Who is sending him back to Egypt? Even in daily life today, a small child may ask, repeatedly, "What is this thing called?" We still intuit that names create reality. It is no accident, therefore, that God creates and names nearly in the same breath. God calls the light Day. God calls the darkness Night. God calls the dome Sky. Adam, would you like to try exercising some of this godlike creative power? Here are some animals. What names will you call them? Parents, you too can have godlike power. Here are your children. What names, formal or informal, will you call them? Spouses, same thing. Names have power. Don't misuse names—especially the name of the Lord.

Names are an important part of creating, though names are not everything. Genesis 2 says God puts people in a garden to till and keep it. How can you be created and truly exist unless you have life-sustaining and dignifying work to do? The first "not good" in the Bible is a solitary human being (Gen 2:18). How can you be created unless you have another person who knows you, who feels a part of you? How can you exist without someone else to hold and behold?

When God begins to create, there is already a physical earth with water, but what kind of earth would you call it? Just a formless void, until God speaks, imparting order and purpose. When God's Spirit moves upon the chaotic face of the deep, then creation can happen with astonishing speed. Suddenly the dry ground is called land, and the land has people to work it, and the people have each other to lie down beside at the end of the day. This is reality we can inhabit.

In short, material existence, which to modern minds seems so obviously to be the focus of Genesis 1 and 2, may not be the focus at all. In this new or ancient reading, creation clearly involves the material realm but also much more. A growing group of Bible teachers has urged the church to hear the opening chapters of Genesis afresh—not as an explanation of chemical or biological origins but rather as an account of God creating real life that is relational. The leading voice for this approach has been John Walton, and what follows draws heavily on his knowledge of ancient languages and literature.[1]

Certainly we don't need detailed knowledge of ancient Near East culture to read the Bible profitably. Walton's critics sometimes accuse him of being a "Gnostic," as if he thinks only his special knowledge unlocks the secrets of the Bible. But I don't think this charge is very fair, for two reasons. First, as I hope to show, many of his insights can be gleaned from a close reading of Scripture itself. Second, the insights that do come from knowledge of cultural context are widely shared with other biblical scholars. This scholarship has its place. Knowledge of cultural contexts can help us recover additional meaning. To take a contemporary example, imagine that someone today were to write these words: "May the force be with you!" Many readers would hear an allusion to popular science fiction. But three thousand years from now, readers might hear only a statement about energy; the allusion to *Star Wars* will have been lost. Similarly, studying cultures from three thousand years ago can enable us to recover lost allusions in Genesis 1. Specifically, these allusions refer to temple construction and inauguration.

Ancient people wrote a lot about their temples, and these writings show a similar pattern. The creation of the temple and the creation of the

---

[1] See especially these two books: John H. Walton, *The Lost World of Genesis One: Ancient Cosmology and the Origins Debate* (Downers Grove, IL: InterVarsity, 2009); and John H. Walton with N. T. Wright, *The Lost World of Adam and Eve: Genesis 2–3 and the Human Origins Debate* (Downers Grove, IL: InterVarsity, 2015).

cosmos often run parallel. The cosmos is the big picture; the temple is the microcosm. People intended their temples to be mini-universes. Hebrew people also thought this way, which is not to say they stole the idea from other cultures. Their thinking grew from their relationship with God, as we see in the Bible. For example, the water basin in the temple built by Solomon is called the "Sea" (1 Kgs 7:25). It must have been a large basin to be called the Sea, but the name also shows how their minds worked: the temple was the cosmos in miniature. Similarly, the tabernacle built by Moses has "lights" that comes from lamps (Exod 25:6), and the same Hebrew word is used to describe the sun and moon on day four of creation (Gen 1:14–17).[2] The cosmos and the temple are interconnected. This idea gets extended in the New Testament book of Hebrews, where the structure of the temple is said to reflect the structure of heaven.

Temple construction and inauguration had two phases, which we learn about in 1 Kings and 2 Chronicles. The building phase came first. It took many tons of physical material to make Solomon's temple—countless cedar logs, stones and precious stones, and vast quantities of silver and gold. It took long hours and arduous labor; the human cost must have been immense. Finally, after all the effort and expense, the construction is finished. But it is not yet a temple. The temple does not yet exist. It has not yet been created. It is only a vast but void physical edifice. The building is waiting to be filled with God's indwelling presence. This indwelling takes place during the temple's inauguration phase. It does not become a temple until it is a home to the God they love.

When the Ark of God's Presence is brought in, the physical space becomes totally transformed. God's glory enters the space and comes upon the people. The cloud of God's Presence is so great "the priests could not stand to minister because of the cloud; for the glory of the Lord filled the house of God" (2 Chr 5:14). The house building took many years. But the inauguration phase, in which the house becomes God's home, is

---

[2] John H. Walton, *The Lost World of Genesis One: Ancient Cosmology and the Origins Debate* (Downers Grove, IL: InterVarsity, 2009), 80.

shorter and more powerful. It happens in the span of just seven days. And the people would think, "Where have we heard this story before?"

Genesis tells about the creation of the macro-temple, the week in which the universe became God's home. God creates by speaking to the physical world, giving it order, purpose, meaning, and divine power to be. This is the week when life on earth begins to become the life of God.

Already, let us suppose, there are physical materials and structures, already plants, animals, and people living and dying, physically speaking. But the entire biological edifice is just a house—not yet a home until God's Spirit sweeps upon the face of the waters and upon the whole earth, turning it into a cosmic temple. Through the act of *bara'*, of creating, the earth is about to become populated with people who are called God's people, and with God's other creatures too.

Let everything that has breath praise the Lord!

CHAPTER 19

Progressive Problems

H ouse and home are a shorthand way to think about the difference between a physical, scientific description and the creation accounts in Genesis. If I were to tell you about our house, I might point out that the construction is brick and wood, while the walls are painted in an off-white semigloss (aka Sherwin-Williams SW 7008 Alabaster). But now imagine you are stepping into our home. The markings on this wall over here show our children's heights, and this little pencil scratch is from the year our son Andrew grew about a foot. We are looking at the same walls, but the focus has shifted.

Walton and others see a similar shift of focus in Genesis, and the proposal before us concerns teaching youth this way of reading Genesis— as an account of relational creation and not of biological or chemical origins. Right away we can see some benefits, as well as some problems, with this proposal.

One large benefit is that it keeps faith and science distinct. It follows the pattern of Chalcedon, which means Genesis no longer gets mixed up or confused with discussions of evolution. Evolutionary biology may be the catalyst that causes us to go back to Genesis to see whether we missed something in our prior understanding. But the evidence for this new and ancient reading is biblical, not scientific. The reading results from comparing various portions of Scripture as well as learning about ancient languages and ancient Near East cultures.

Just as this reading stands or falls on biblical evidence, so too neo-Darwinian theories must stand or fall on scientific evidence. One can accept (or reject) those theories with or without accepting this reading of Genesis. Neo-Darwinian evolution focuses exclusively on material causes and physical origins, whereas this reading of Genesis shifts the focus to the spiritual sphere. This reading is not based on a fear of conflict with science but instead a desire to hear God's message to the original audience and to us today.

A second benefit for Christians is that this reading connects life in Genesis with the meaning of life in the New Testament. Discussions of Darwin do little to help us understand the "life" that is in Jesus, whereas this reading lets us connect Genesis with the Gospel of John: both are talking about the source of true and abundant life. This reading also helps us make connections within Genesis itself. Building on Walton, we can hear how the first twelve chapters overall depict the call of God. We hear God calling Abraham and Sarah from among the scattered peoples; God calling Noah and Naamah (his wife, according to midrash) from among the disobedient populace; God calling Adam and Eve from the dust of mortality; God calling light out of darkness.

A third benefit, for some readers, is that this proposal lets us take Genesis not just seriously but also literally. It lets us affirm, if we choose, that God literally created the cosmos in the span of seven days, and each day was twenty-four hours long, and all this creative activity could have taken place around six or seven thousand years ago. But first, we need to grasp that "create" (*bara'*) literally meant *relational* creation to the people who first heard God's Word.

Along with these benefits, this proposal brings some problems. First, some verses in Genesis certainly seem to be talking about acts of material creation. What are we to make of God forming Adam out of dust or Eve out of Adam's rib? Second, we have the letters of Paul, which seem to state outright that Adam was the first human being and furthermore that

Adam's sin was the start of physical death on earth. These passages cannot be overlooked but must be examined closely.

Before doing so, however, a third problem calls for attention: people in your church may feel disinclined to reread anything and especially Genesis. Some churches are tired of talking about evolution and creation, while others may get energized by it, but in either case, most have settled on an approach that seems to work for them.

Talk to one group of church leaders, and they will say, "We teach our youth to read Genesis figuratively. Not everything in the Bible is meant to be taken literally. The Bible is wrong about some things because it was written by people who did not have science to tell them how nature really works, but thankfully these errors are not essential to faith. Mainly, we want our youth to know that there is no conflict between Christian faith and modern science. Otherwise they may leave church and not come back."

I think this approach does not actually work as well as its proponents think it does.

Talk to another group of church leaders, and they will say, "We teach our youth to read Genesis literally. There is a very clear conflict between God's Word and a 'molecules to man' theory of evolution. We want our young people to trust the former, so they must learn early on why the latter is wrong. Mainly, we want our youth to know the Bible is reliable. Otherwise they may leave church and not come back."

I think this approach also does not actually work as well as its proponents think it does.

The motives are commendable—retaining young people, defending faith, resolving conflicts between faith and science. But the routes are wrong, or at least not the best. In letting evolution set the stage for reading Genesis, both approaches keep the focus too much on the physical realm. To pave the way for rereading through eyes of the heart, I will risk alienating some readers by critiquing these current approaches to teaching youth about Genesis.

Take the figurative reading first. The words *figurative* and *not literal* often appear in teaching that follows a science-says trajectory. It goes something like this. Before science, ancient people made up stories or myths about how the earth was formed. They all did it, and they all got it wrong. The ancient Hebrews, for example, thought the sky was a dome made of metal, because sturdy material was required to hold back the vast pool of "waters above the earth"—and amusingly to our ears, they thought the metal dome had tiny holes to let down raindrops. This naive mindset is what gave rise to the creation stories in Genesis. They did the best they could, but they did not have modern science. We do, so we can no longer take these stories or myths literally. Instead, we ought to read them figuratively.

A tentative hand goes up. What does exactly this mean—to read it "figuratively"?

Good question. Figurative could mean we look for ethical content. Genesis says to take good care of the earth, still a sound principle today. Or else figurative could mean pondering existential possibilities. Like other classics of literature, these stories depict the human condition, causing us to reflect more deeply on it. Or figurative could mean we glean the story for some basic theological point—for instance, the idea that God is somehow in back of the process we now call evolution.

Whatever figurative means, the important thing is that it does not mean literal or factual. With this approach, youth leaders can reassure their charges that one does not need to believe everything in the Bible "word for word." Even if some earlier audiences read these stories that way, today's youth require and deserve a more enlightened approach.

This summary of a science-says approach may resonate with some readers. It may contain ideas that many of us have been teaching our youth, ideas we learned from our freethinking elders. These ideas are part of an important story or myth of our own times, told repeatedly around our figurative campfires. It is the story or myth of modernity.

The modern myth has grains of truth but also potent seeds of error. For one thing, it puts us in a position of cultural superiority. It says we know vastly more than earlier people or people living in less "advanced" societies today. And certainly we do, and this much is true: feelings of cultural superiority are fully warranted, so long as we are talking about science and technology. But science is not all of reality. There are some nonscientific dimensions of reality that the ancient Hebrews and early Christians could possibly have seen better than we, through eyes of the heart. In fact, our scientific and technological superiority may sometimes occlude our spiritual vision. It may, for instance, cause us to read Genesis as a primitive and outdated attempt to explain the physical world instead of seeing it as a timely window into the spiritual realm.

Therefore, the first major problem with the science-says approach is that it looks at Genesis through eyes of science rather than eyes of the heart. By focusing on physical creation in Genesis, it reinforces our present spiritual impoverishment. It supports the modern assumption that the physical is the most real, and it fuels the modern suspicion that the spiritual realm of love, joy, and peace may just be a function and fiction of the human brain.

The second major problem with the science-says approach is the process for getting there. The process summons a mental technology that, once deployed, becomes hard to control. In the previous century, this mental process gained the name "demythologizing," which meant reading biblical accounts as myths from which the modern reader can extract ethical values, existential options, or poetic themes. The actual facts do not matter so long as we grasp the deeper truth of the narrative—so it was said. We recognize it is a problem when political opponents accuse each other of fudging the facts to fit the "truth" of their narratives. So why should we think facts are irrelevant in the religious sphere? After all, our science-saturated culture is teaching youth that the realm of the actual and factual, the realm of the material and historical, is the most real of all, so at the least we may expect some confusion if we tell youth to disregard facts in the Bible.

This issue is a bit complicated, since facts are filtered through mental lenses, and context does matter. At the start of this chapter, I spoke of pencil scratches on the wall of our home and of one particular scratch showing the year our son Andrew grew about a foot. What if his growth was actually 6.3 inches? Further, I need to confess that these scratches do not actually exist in our home. Walls take a lot of time to paint, so we try not to mark them up with pencils (though children have their own ideas). In a scientific article, these factual errors would be fatal flaws, but hopefully in this context, the reader will allow that the illustration was fabricated to explain the difference between a house and a home.

Returning to the Bible, we could have a discussion, say, about numbers. Are large numbers in the Bible to be understood as actual facts conforming to our modern scientific sensibility, or are they being used to make a point about greatness and importance? In a traditional approach to answering this question, the church would read and pray for the guidance of the Holy Spirit. The church would then examine the text and also look at the context in which the words were written.

However, in a science-says approach, our present-day context becomes the arbiter. From our scientific vantage point, what do we think is possible or realistic? This mindset can too easily bulldoze aside the sense of believers around the world and down through the ages; it can suppress the desire to be guided by the Holy Spirit. Instead, our scientifically informed "common sense" tells us what to believe. Jesus says to love our enemies. Yes, but you can't always take the Bible literally. The Bible says Jesus was born of a virgin and that he rose from the dead after three days. Yes, but you can't believe everything word for word. Once set in motion, the mental process of demythologizing is hard to control.

No one would claim that every part of the Bible is historical fact. Parables and poetry are woven into the canon, and terms like *figurative* and *symbolic* are good to have at our disposal when reading the Bible. But once upon a time, symbols had numinous power; they were seen as the most real instantiation of something. The problem with a "figurative" reading today is that it gets wedded to a science-says stance and perpetuates in young minds a two-tiered sense of reality. Science tells us what is real and true for everyone. The rest is stories and opinions. Bible stories are good. They are like watching movies or a good series. You find the ones you like. You exit the narrative once you lose interest or feel offended. Everyone gets to pick and choose and decide for themselves.

In sum, the foregoing approach may help young people to resolve conflicts between Genesis and evolution, but it comes at a cost. By keeping the focus on material creation, it forecloses spiritual insight. If we have two competing accounts of material origins, evolution and creation, then we have on the one hand the right answer, which is scientific, and on the other, some ancient stories that a young person may or may not find interesting today. In the end, this approach may promote what it seeks to prevent. We can expect young people to leave church when they find other creative and artistic outlets to be more personally engaging than church.

This critique of progressive teaching is not, however, a defense of the Bible-says approach taken by many young-earth and old-earth creationists. The pitfalls of creationism are discussed in the next chapter.

CHAPTER 20

Creationism

A science-says approach, common among progressive Christians, is willing to let science decide all physical and most metaphysical questions, provided the church is permitted to continue its mission of compassion and social justice. By contrast, conservative Christians, who are more apt to take a Bible-says approach, are usually ready to oppose science when it conflicts with their faith. This faith rests squarely on the Bible's reliability, starting with the first words: "In the beginning God created."

When these Christians reject neo-Darwinian evolution, they still maintain that good science and the Bible will always agree. Their battle is not against science per se but against mainstream scientists who have reached consensus on issues such as the age of the earth and the origins of human life. With just two premises in place—(1) Genesis is an account of material origins, and (2) good science and the Bible will always agree—the stage is set for a recurring drama. The pattern of the drama goes like this. First, as a creationist, I assert the Bible says x. Second, scientific evidence opposed to x reaches a tipping point. Third, in response, I assert with equal force that the Bible says y. What remains constant in these shifting interpretations is the Bible's inerrancy.

We can plug in some variables. For a long time, people read the Bible and thought the creation accounts meant the earth was young. Then geologists in the eighteenth century determined the earth was old, and gradually this idea gained wide acceptance. In response, conservative Bible teachers set forth a new reading of Genesis known as "gap creationism." This new reading claimed that God accomplished two distinct creations, and it required the reader's mind to insert a gap of several million years between the first and second verses of Genesis: "In the beginning, God created the heavens and the earth [and then, millions of years later] the earth was a formless void [so God started to create things a second time]." The gap between the first and second creations grew much wider after scientists increased the age of the earth from millions to billions of years.

The gap was not totally pointless. It allowed ample time for Satan to be created and then rebel, along with a percentage of other angels, and overall many Bible believers found this reading to be an elegant solution to a potential conflict between faith and science. Gap creationism was promoted in the reference notes of the influential 1917 *Scofield Reference Bible.*

It seems obvious this new understanding of Genesis did not come from a plain reading of the text, but rather it was a rereading in response to scientific evidence. It gained favor because it allowed churches to teach their youth that the existence of a very old earth does not erode biblical authority in the least. In fact, Genesis itself, if read correctly, tells us the earth is very old. God knew it was old before scientists did because God created it, and God basically wrote the Bible. In short, though creationism had once assumed a young earth, it now asserted with equal force that the earth is old, just as the Bible says.

Gap creationism lost a lot of steam after the 1950s with the advent of the modern young-earth creation movement, which promoted a different message. In effect, this view said scientists had been fooled. God made a fully mature-looking universe and earth with the *appearance* of age built in—just as Adam and Eve started life as grown-ups, and just as the trees in the garden were not saplings but had fruit-bearing branches right from the start. In this view, Genesis, if read correctly, once again tells us the earth is very young. (By contrast, Walton's proposal introduced in chapter 18 says that Genesis, if read correctly, tells us nothing about the earth's age.)

Young-earth creationists see the battle for biblical authority as being waged in the fields of science, particularly the key issues of evolution and the age of the earth. After breakthroughs in genetics changed the course of mainstream evolutionary biology, creationists in turn changed their counterarguments to keep pace. Amid change, some tenets remained stable: a young earth, a global flood, and a firm conviction that Adam and Eve could not have descended from earlier life-forms. But in defending these tenets, young-earth creationists have shown a remarkable willingness to adapt.

Leading organizations (at the time of this writing), such as Answers in Genesis, the Institute for Creation Research, and Creation Ministries International, serve their constituents by trying to stay apprised of mainstream science developments in order to supply more up-to-date counterarguments. No one can doubt their zeal, for at the same time they seek to oppose the entire edifice of mainstream biology, they must fight additional side battles—against old-earth creationists, against each other over issues such as funding, and against fringe voices infiltrating their cause to proclaim seriously that the earth is flat, that NASA faked the moon landing, or some other eyebrow-raising idea equally removed from reality. That outliers can give rise to even more radical fringes should surprise no one; the same dynamic is found in all arenas of social, political, and religious life.

What *is* surprising, however, is the degree to which young-earth creationists have been willing to revise their arguments in response to mainstream science. Standard debating points of yesteryear—for example, that evolution is just a theory, that there are no transitional forms, and that there is an amazing amount of scientific insight in the Bible—are now found verbatim on lists of now-outdated arguments that young people are advised *not* to use.[1]

---

[1] "Arguments We Think Creationists Should NOT Use," answers to "What arguments are doubtful, hence inadvisable to use?," Creation Ministries International, https://tinyurl.com/yarmlwbl.

The following "catechism," which I have drawn from creationist curricula, demonstrates the extent to which creationist arguments have evolved.

Do young-earth creationists reject evolution?

No. They agree that scientific evolution simply means change in heritable traits over successive generations.

So then, do young-earth creationists accept micro-evolution but reject macro-evolution?

No. This distinction was once crucial to their case. It meant you could accept the existence of small adaptations, such as the changing shape of finch beaks, without agreeing that new phyla emerged over billions of years. But today, leading creationists think the term *macro-evolution* is too fuzzy to be useful and the whole discussion is a distraction from a new focus on genetic information.

Do young-earth creationists assert there are no beneficial mutations?

No. They now teach youth that some mutations do confer a survival advantage.

Do young-earth creationists think no new species have been produced since the days of Genesis?

No. More recent creation science curriculum teaches the opposite: "In fact, *rapid* speciation is an important part of the creation model. But this speciation is within the 'kind' and involves no new genetic information" (italics original).[2]

Here we come to the crux of the current (at time of this writing) stance of young-earth creationists. It hinges on two things: a new translation of one word in Genesis and a new focus on genetics.

The word *min* (מִין), or "kind," occurs ten times in the first chapter of Genesis. All things are created according to their kinds. Problems arise as soon as we try to correlate "kind" with scientific terminology. The word cannot mean species because land-based species alone number about 6.5 million, a much greater quantity than could fit within the confines of

---

[2] *Answers Academy: Biblical Apologetics for Real Life*, participant's workbook (Petersburg, KY: Answers in Genesis, 2018), 35.

Noah's ark. Creationists are today careful to clarify that *min* does not mean species. One handbook says it "probably" correlates with "a classification rank somewhere around family and order. In other words, Noah would have brought two representatives from the cat family, not two tigers, two lions, and two ocelots."[3] This translation greatly reduces the number of ark occupants but also greatly increases the need for post-flood variation—hence the newfound embrace of evolutionary mechanisms. Today's creationists believe not only in evolution but in extremely rapid evolution of a sort requiring much divine assistance.

I personally would not advise telling young people that "kind" correlates with family, order, class, phylum, or any other term from zoology. I have recommended a Chalcedonian pattern for relating science and Christian faith. From this standpoint, mixing biblical language with scientific taxonomy creates confusion. Words have different meanings in different contexts, and the spiritually charged thought world of the Bible differs from the thought world of material-minded scientists.

Young-earth creationists have been especially inclined to bring scientific terms into discussions of Genesis. They want to defend the eternal truth of God's Word against perceived attacks from human knowledge in the form of science. However, as we have just seen, this defense must continually pivot to keep pace with science, which can cause confusion in young minds. Whatever its problems, one distinct advantage of Walton's proposal is that it shifts the focus from the biological sphere and thus inoculates Genesis from scientific attack. It is a defense of God's Word that does not require continual updates or plug-ins. It lets the word "kind" (*min*) dwell in its own thought world.

And yet, though I am critical of the young-earth creationists' approach, I am very sympathetic to their overriding concern. They are trying to help youth bring together the world of faith and the world of science. That the two worlds have been rent apart is the whole reason for writing this book. There needs to be a union without confusion between faith and science.

[3] Nathaniel T. Jeanson, "What Happened to the Animals after Noah's Ark? Stepping Back in Time," Answers in Genesis: The Origin of Species after the Flood, June 11, 2016, https://tinyurl.com/ydfc5cnx.

Creationism can cause confusion when it slips back and forth between the material evidence of science and the invisible evidence of faith, when it cites a scientific study in one breath and quotes Scripture in the next. But still, at the end of the day, there does need to be a union of faith and science, enabling a coherent worldview. And this is what young-earth creationists are trying to achieve.

Also commendable is a more recent trajectory of creationist discourse. As more people with advanced science training have entered the movement, its rhetorical tone has softened. One reads less often the charge that evolutionary biology is the single worst lie perpetrated by Satan. Instead, young people are taught to be more measured about mainstream science and to press their case using scientific terminology. One should not flatly declare that "there are no beneficial mutations" (since some mutations do confer a survival benefit). Instead, one should say, "We have yet to find a mutation that increases genetic information, even in those rare instances where the mutation confers an advantage."[4]

The content of this assertion aside, one can hear a scientific sensibility in these words: "we have yet to find." The process of scientific exploration is always ongoing. Whatever its origins, young-earth creationism has been evolving in an age of science.

Given recent developments, we ought to be clear about the kind of evolution that today's creationists oppose. It is not, as we have said, theories of evolution in general. It is not micro- or macro-evolution. Rather, they now say they oppose "molecules-to-man" or "particles-to-people" evolution. This position is not totally untenable. Most scientists would probably agree "we have yet to find" the pathways by which the mechanisms of evolution can produce the whole continuum from particles to people.

The beginning and the end of this process—the emergence of the first living cells at the start and the emergence of human consciousness at the end—have proved especially elusive. Scientists have tried to devise laboratory conditions that mimic the transition from inorganic matter to living cells in order to explain how self-reproducing molecules came

---

[4] *Answers Academy: Biblical Apologetics for Real Life*, participant's workbook, 35.

to be—the start of the process. They would like to be able to produce computer models that show how evolutionary mechanisms can give rise to human consciousness—the end of the process (from a human perspective). But cells and consciousness are both incredibly complex, and these goals are currently unmet. Scientists are still looking, though they have yet to find.

Proponents of "intelligent design" will say most scientists are looking in the wrong direction. Physical life is now understood largely in terms of genetic information. To many people living in an information age, it makes intuitive sense that the genetic information needed for physical life would originate from a designing Mind, not from particles of matter. By analogy, computer information comes from intelligence, not silicon.

Most biologists consider Intelligent Design a pseudo-science. Intelligent Design faces the problem of guilt by association; it is seen as an offshoot of young-earth creationism, even though the ideas of Intelligent Design predate the modern creationist movement by two centuries. However, creationists have worked to have Intelligent Design included in public school biology curricula, which fuels the impression that Intelligent Design is simply creationism in disguise.

Whatever its appeal to engineers, computer scientists, or mathematicians, Intelligent Design has always been a square peg among biologists, since the days when Darwin rebuked Wallace for his Intelligent Design inclinations. Modern biologists especially do not appreciate people from other fields telling them how to do their jobs. Their response, in effect, has been "Go home and develop your own research program instead of coming here to poke holes in ours. We can find the holes easily enough on our own."

Intelligent Design proponents will say they are in fact developing research programs, but they have the unenviable job of trying to convince people with years of physical science training to rebuild their whole enterprise on a nonphysical foundation. The argument did not meet with success back in the nineteenth century when it involved pocket watches and eyeballs; perhaps it will fare better with silicon chips and DNA. But at any rate, Intelligent Design cannot currently help us bring faith and science together. Its aspiration to become an accepted program of modern science means it must exclude any whiff of biblical faith.

We can sum up the problems with a creationist Bible-says approach to teaching Genesis. Like the science-says approach just discussed, it keeps the focus trained on the physical realm. It strives to defend the Bible's trustworthiness, but this defense responds to science with shifting biblical interpretations, which in turn cause confusion among congregations and internal squabbles among experts (e.g., old-earth creationists versus young-earth creationists).

The struggles within and without are not without benefit. Youth who are taught creationism are more likely to know the terms of evolutionary biology than youth in a science-says church, in the same way that people who oppose vaccinations are more likely to know the ingredients of a vaccine. But for creationist Ken Ham and others, the greater goal is not increased interest in science but a decreased flow of young people leaving Bible-believing churches.

From a sociological perspective, this flow is not as fast as they may fear, though movement *between* conservative churches has become much more common. Of course, even one lost sheep is too many, especially if it is your own child. However, pitting biblical authority against the most influential scientific theory of the past two centuries places a severe burden on young minds. And in some cases, it may actually hasten the result its teachers had hoped to avoid. At least some young adults will say they left their Bible-believing church because it opposed science. Case in point: evolutionary biology.

All of which brings us back to Walton's proposal—a literal reading of Genesis that reclaims an original meaning of the word *bara'* (create), that allows Adam and Eve to be both archetypal and actual people, and that permits harmony with biological evolution. To some Bible-believing ears, this solution may sound too good. What's the catch? The catch is all the verses in Genesis and Romans we have not yet talked about. Addressing some of these sticking points should be interesting, even to readers who long ago made their peace with evolutionary biology, for it will draw us into the fertile depth of Christian theology.

CHAPTER 21

A Handful of Dust

A small child can pick up a handful of loose dirt and watch it sift slowly through her fingers. A child can also picture God taking dirt and making clay, then shaping it into a person, and then—in a moment of truth—breathing life into this newly fashioned form. Behold, the first human being!

This mental picture of God creating Adam is entirely wrong, says John Walton. He bases his case not on Darwin but on Hebrew. "Then the Lord God formed man from the dust of the ground, and breathed into his nostrils the breath of life; and the man became a living being" (Gen 2:7). Walton argues the original audience of Genesis would never have supposed God was making a material person from scratch. Instead, they would have heard an account of God endowing a mere mortal with divine purpose and power.

Walton sets out to dismantle the material image, word by word. Though "formed" (Hebrew *ysr*) sounds like a material act, it is not necessarily that. When God forms the heart (Ps 33:15) or forms future events (2 Kgs 19:25) or forms our days on earth (Ps 139:16), we can see how the word *form* does not need to entail any manipulation of material molecules. Walton cites other instances where "formed" in the Bible is not a physical act.

Some of these examples are admittedly ambiguous. What Walton calls "one of the clearest examples" is to my mind one of the least clear. The

Lord "forms [*ysr*] the human spirit within a person," says Zechariah 12:1, and Walton notes, "Here the direct object of the verb ['forms'] is the human spirit, which is categorically not material." Yes, in Christian theology, but Walton wants to reclaim the original Hebrew understanding, and as he well knows but does not here discuss, the Hebrew word for spirit also means breath—and breath of the sort you can see before your face on a cold morning, which categorically *is* material.

But let's allow for now that "formed" in Genesis 2:7 does not compel a material understanding. Surely "dust" does—or does it? Walton argues, in slow and deliberate steps, that it does not. If we want to think physically, then we must agree the main ingredient in a human body is water, not dust. Further, if the verse were talking about God's hands-on craftsmanship, we would expect the word *clay*, since clay is malleable, whereas dust is not. Most important, the next chapter of Genesis spells out just what "dust" does mean. To the Hebrew mind, it means mortality: "You are dust, and to dust you shall return" (Gen 3:17).

Several other places in the Bible reinforce this idea that dust stands for mortality. If "forming from dust" were a statement about material origins, then it would apply only to Adam, but Psalm 103:14 speaks of everyone in this vein:

> For God knows how we were made;
> he remembers that we are dust.

One can anticipate a counterargument that dust becomes an image for mortality precisely because it is the essential physical ingredient (just add water) of the first mortal. However, if we are willing to give Walton's new or ancient focus a fair hearing, we find it is not unfaithful to the rest of Scripture. Let's proceed.

As for Adam, so for Eve. Her creation is also not physical—not the result of a surgical operation that extracts Adam's rib. Along with Jewish scholars from centuries ago, Walton proposes that "side" is a much better translation than rib. The "deep sleep" refers to a mystical vision (akin to Peter's sleep in Acts) whereby God reveals to Adam that man and woman are created to be ontologically side by side. They are connected and complementary.

Walton thus argues that Genesis 2 is no more an account of physical origins than Genesis 1 is. The first audience would have heard a story of God giving order, meaning, and purpose to preexistent physical life. On this reading, Adam and Eve are not the first people. But they are the first to be called God's people. They are "the first *significant* humans," says Walton.[1]

Building on Walton's insights, we can tell the story this way. In the first chapter of Genesis, God created the earth to become a temple. In the second chapter, God chooses two people to be the first priests. Starting with Adam and Eve, the human vocation is to receive creation as a gift from God and offer it back to God. Starting with them, the human temptation is to take and consume creation apart from God.

As well as being the first priests, Adam and Eve are also the first king and queen. Here is another place where it helps to know the cultural context. In literature of surrounding cultures, kings were another popular topic. Kings, like priests, were seen as the gods' representatives on earth. Often king and priest were the same person. Kings—but only kings—were said to possess the gods' "likeness" or the gods' "image." Genesis 1 tells a different story. God intends all humanity to have this high vocation of being royalty, starting with Adam and Eve ("in the image of God . . . he created them"). Adam and Eve are given dominion over creation, meaning they should use their God-given power for God-given purposes. Even in surrounding literature, good kings were said to rule with justice and mercy. The Bible later speaks of all Israel as being a "royal priesthood," and the New Testament applies this idea to Christ and to the Christian calling. The priestly and royal vocation first given to Adam and Eve is made perfect in Christ and thus restored to humanity.

Names, we recall, are important in creation. Adam's name literally means Man (or Earthling). Eve means Living. Despite their archetypal-sounding names, Walton personally holds that Adam and Eve were actual

---

[1] John H. Walton with N. T. Wright, *The Lost World of Adam and Eve: Genesis 2–3 and the Human Origins Debate* (Downers Grove, IL: InterVarsity, 2015), 114.

people who lived in the ancient Near East. His position safeguards the physicality of Jesus's genealogy in Luke (which dates back to Adam), and it also obviates the troubling question of when Genesis moves from being nonhistorical to becoming historical. It is historical throughout, with all the standard scholarly qualifications of what "history" meant to ancient people. Adam and Eve were two people with whom you could shake hands or exchange fist bumps.

But due to their names, and for other reasons, Walton believes even more strongly that Adam and Eve are also archetypes. In fact, their on-going identity as archetypes matters much more than their place in history. He takes several chapters to explain why both an original Hebrew audience and the later New Testament writers would have viewed Adam and Eve in this manner—as archetypes who represent the vocation and temptation of all humanity, not as biological progenitors of the species we now call *Homo sapiens*.

The idea that Adam and Eve are created while other *Homo sapiens* were milling about Mesopotamia will sound strange to many Christian readers. But this idea was not strange to their son Cain. As he is about to be cast into exile for murdering his brother Abel, Cain complains, "I will be a restless wanderer on the earth, and whoever finds me will kill me" (Gen 4:14 NIV). He anticipates encountering hostile strangers, so the Lord puts a protective mark on Cain. The logical inference is that the land east of Eden had been populated by people other than Adam and Eve.

Here we return to Einstein's remark that the theory decides what we are able to see. If our theory says that Adam and Eve were the sole biological progenitors of all humanity, then we must reject the natural reading of this verse, which clearly implies foreigners had settled east of Eden. The theory that Adam and Eve are the first and only humans compels us to construct a different scenario, in which incest becomes part of God's original design for humankind. Once past this significant hurdle, some quick math enables us to speculate that Cain's brothers and sisters had enough time to get married, leave home, settle east of Eden, and populate the land with potential enemies of the exiled Cain.

Then comes another obstacle. People in Old Testament cultures are very attentive to genealogies and family relations. Yet Cain does not say, "My relatives will kill me." Nor does the Lord say, "On second thought, Cain, instead of this mark, why don't you just remind those hostile strangers that you are their father or grandfather, their uncle, brother, or cousin."

The underlying question is still whether God, in creating Adam and Eve, is arranging material molecules or doing relational creation. If the theory says arranging material molecules, then this reading drives us to think that Adam and Eve are the first and only biological people, and we are forced to accept a narrative of propagation by incest. The theory of relational creation avoids this and other problems. Cain's complaint actually makes more plain sense if Adam and Eve are the first priests, not the first people per se.

Nothing the Old Testament says about Adam and Eve contradicts the idea that other *Homo sapiens* were living at the same time. In fact, after the initial chapters of Genesis, the Old Testament says very little about the primal pair. Adam is mentioned only twice, and Eve not at all. One of the references to Adam is the start of a genealogy; the second reference is ambiguous, in that it could also be speaking about a town named Adam.

But Adam and Eve regain considerable prominence in the New Testament and in subsequent Christian art and literature. One can easily picture the primal pair: he gazes upon her as she gazes upon the apple held aloft in her hand, while nearby a cobra coils around the trunk of some ancient tree. Alone in the universe, they are poised between innocence and guilt. Christian children see these sorts of images growing up, and it affects how we read the Bible.

When I was a child, the church service on Christmas Eve was a series of Bible readings interspersed with Christmas carols. The first reading was always about Adam and Eve. Every year, the story of Jesus's birth began with their fall. Cosmic fall and cosmic redemption became a grand narrative in which single concrete acts—the bite of the fruit, the nails on the cross, the personal prayer of surrender—have eternal consequences.

I certainly don't want to lose this narrative or its grandeur. But is it not enough to claim that Adam and Eve are where the story begins for us? Must we also insist that no other biological people existed before them?

Some readers will say yes, we must so insist, because this is the picture Paul gives us in the New Testament. So we will turn to Paul next. But first, let's pause to weigh the benefit of reading Genesis as relational creation. If the creation narrative is not a physical explanation in competition with science, then it can become more fully a spiritual account that offers what modern science can never supply: the story of why we are here.

To ancient Hebrews and early Christians, having existence or being—to be created—meant having order, purpose, and meaning to your life. It meant you had a name and occupation, a land on which to live and a family to call your own. It meant, above all, being in relationality with God and with everything else created by God. Creation meant being integrally connected to the earth ("dust") and intimately connected to one another ("rib"). Dust to dust. Bone of my bone. This ancient understanding feels as timely now as ever.

We live in an age of science but also an era of disconnection and alienation. Youth today are more scientifically advanced and technologically advantaged than any generation in history. In America, they enjoy overall an unprecedented standard of living, economically speaking. Yet many suffer—and suffer does seem to be the right word—from anxiety, depression, feelings of worthlessness, fear of loneliness, thoughts of suicide. Whatever the brain-chemical components of these maladies, people in ministry can see an aching spiritual need.

If in adolescence, which is often the first season of intense self-consciousness, they rely solely on modern science to supply their creation story, the message falls short. Your life is the result of a random process. Who am I? You are at root a mind-boggling mass of molecules clustered in and around a brain and central nervous system. Layer on top of this metaphysical (or anti-metaphysical) foundation all the feelings of being homeless and rootless that modern technological mobility has intensified, and we have a "house of being" that may look economically stable but in all reality is built on lifeless sand and dust. The house is waiting to become a home where God takes up residence.

For Christians, Genesis offers a vision of this home at the cosmic level. Creation in Genesis is a big picture of God-ordered life, even as creation in John shows us that the origin and locus of this life is Jesus—"in him was life" (John 1:4). In sum, the relational reading of Genesis offers more spiritual sustenance for youth today than the biological reading. Walton and others contend it is also the accurate reading; it is how the first audience of Genesis would have heard the creation narratives. Whereas we think of life in biological terms, they understood life in relational and spiritual terms.

Not only life but also death is an important topic to teach young people. The Bible speaks frequently of death. While every thread in Genesis—Cain's mark, Adam's rib, Eve's name—unravels a skein of meaning, probably the most poignant phrase of all is God's warning to the new couple: "In the day you eat of the fruit, you shall die." What kind of day and what kind of death are we talking about here?

The Medicine of Immortality

W hy do people still die?

This question came to me, as it might to any young believer, upon reading the New Testament. The question is theological, not biological, and it grows more pressing after the loss—that is, the death—of someone close. "Our Savior Christ Jesus has abolished death and brought life and immortality to light" (2 Tim 1:10). If Christ abolished death, why did Grandpa die?

The New Testament itself probes this question, and various verses have been juxtaposed to frame the problem in terms of "already" and "not yet." Already Christ is risen, the first fruits and foretaste of what is to come. Not yet have all dead-and-buried Christians been resurrected. Already the devil is rendered powerless to keep people in fear of death. Not yet has the faith that overcomes this fear been made sight. Already the spiritual reality of death as separation from God is swallowed up in victory. Not yet has death's physical reality been abolished; physical death is the "last enemy to be destroyed" (1 Cor 15:26).

This framework of "already" and "not yet" provides coherence for reading the New Testament epistles. But it does not really answer the question: Why the long time delay (why any time delay) between the bodily resurrection of Jesus and the end to physical death on earth? Two theologians of the past century offered me helpful insights into this mystery.

For those who like to think historically, Wolfhart Pannenberg spoke of Christ's resurrection as the end of history breaking into the middle of history. His resurrection outside Jerusalem is a sneak preview of what will happen for all people everywhere at the end of time. In the meantime, there is still more history to accomplish—still more life, love, and work on earth to be done. We can participate more energetically because we have glimpsed the happy ending.

A second insight comes from Orthodox theologian Alexander Schmemann. In writing about baptism, Schmemann urges the church to see that water baptism is our own death and resurrection, literally and not just figuratively. By baptism we are included in the death and resurrection of Jesus (Rom 6:3–5). The spiritual reality of Christ's death and resurrection—and of our union with him in these events—is more real than the lingering phenomenon of physical death. But then why *does* physical death still linger? Schmemann answers:

> [Christ] does not "abolish" or "destroy" the physical death because He does not abolish *this world* in which physical death is not only a "part" but the principle of life and even growth. But He does infinitely more. By removing the sting of sin from death, by abolishing death as a spiritual reality, by filling it with Himself, with His love and life, He makes [physical] death—which was the very reality of separation and corruption of life—into a shining and joyful "passage"—passover—into fuller life, fuller communion, fuller love. "For to me to live is Christ," says St. Paul, "and to die is gain" (Phil. 1:21).

This is modern Byzantine theology in the tradition of Paul, whereby the worst is transformed into the best. Physical death had once spelled abject separation, but Christ transforms physical death, turning it into a shining passage to fuller life. Balancing this joyful proclamation with sympathy for those who are grieving is vital to pastoral ministry.

Most pertinent to the question at hand, Schmemann remarks that physical death is intrinsic to this physical universe. Without physical death, broadly speaking (death of cells, people, plants, animals, and so forth), there could be no flourishing of physical life on earth. On this earth, physical death and physical life are intertwined. And on this biological fact, Orthodox theologians, atheistic evolutionists, and young-earth creationists can all agree. But the follow-up question becomes, Was it always thus?

In other words, did God intend from the start a physical universe in which physical death is an intrinsic part and even a principle of life and growth? Or was physical death rather a direct result of human sin? The second option is what many young believers learn when the gospel is first explained to them. Adam and Eve are disobedient in eating from a tree, and physical death enters the world for the first time. Jesus Christ is obedient by dying on a "tree," and physical death is expelled from the world. The parallel is elegant, if not exact, given the problem just named—that physical death has not yet been expelled.

But in general, this is the cosmic history that many young Christians hold: in God's original design, before the fall, people were exempt from physical death, and so too were many other species. In this view, the disobedient bite of the fruit was the cataclysm that turned immortals into mortals. A view so widely embraced is not easily dismissed. There is something to be said for strength in numbers. At the same time, this view has problems, both biological and biblical.

The biological problems are that (a) it makes absolutely no sense to most professional biologists, and (b) even for believers who accept that God can easily configure the physical world any which way, two nagging questions remain. One question concerns the food chain. How many organisms were placed high enough on it to qualify for immortality before the fall? It would seem we could let plants and other vegetation die and get eaten easily enough, thus reserving pre-fall immortality for animals with whom we feel some affinity. Except it needs to be noted that studies show how mother plants grow in ways that favor their children and close relatives over plants that are more distant relatives. Parent plants, when traumatized, pass on the effects, which are manifest in their offspring.

A discussion of plant feelings may seem far afield, but these are exactly the kind of issues that teenagers are likely to raise, because they are coming of age intellectually and testing the limits of logic. To respond prematurely, "Well, you just have to have faith," may unwittingly send the signal that Christian faith is not for the smarter kids. It is valid to ask, "Exactly who and what did not die before the fall, and why?"

The theory of no death before the fall presents an even larger question of how appetites, digestive tracts, and other biological apparatus become instantly reconstructed after the first human transgression so that previously peaceful animals suddenly start to devour one another. This question is as much biblical as it is biological. Why does Genesis make no mention of such a momentous event? God speaks of the ground producing thorns and thistles and of human labor becoming arduous. But nowhere do we read of herbivores becoming carnivores, and nowhere, frankly, does it state that animals were ever immortal. Nowhere, on close reading, does it say people were immortal. It *does* say that God said, "On the day you eat of it, you will die."

Here is a different and more literal interpretation. On the literal, twenty-four-hour day they disobey, they do die—and in the way that matters most: in relationship to God. So long as they were willing to find their life in God, they had access to the tree of life, which was true life, divine life, and also life without end. But Eve and Adam decide to consume life on their own terms. By eating from the tree of good and evil, they learn about evil by doing it, and having done it, they lose the power of choosing otherwise. Evil has an addictive quality.

Sin spelled separation and spiritual death, whereupon the mortal body began to fall back to its original limits. Dust began to return to dust. They lost the immortality that came from communion with God. In short, the tree of good and evil did not turn immortals into mortals. Rather, the tree of life had enabled mortals to become immortal.

This is one place where Walton's exegesis of the Bible connects with strands of Eastern Orthodox theology. Walton argues that the first Hebrew audience would never have thought Adam and Eve were immortal before the fall. After all, people who are inherently immortal do not need a tree of life.[1] But precisely because they *are* mortal, God gives them death's

---

[1] Walton, *The Lost World of Adam and Eve*, 74.

antidote. In the first century of Christian history, Ignatius of Antioch described the Eucharist as the "medicine of immortality"; these words are sung weekly by Orthodox Christians today, in the liturgy of Saint John Chrysostom. This phrase "medicine of immortality" also aptly describes the tree of life.

When Adam and Eve are driven from the garden, they lose access to their source of immortality. God places not just barbed wire but terrifying angels with flaming swords in front of the tree of life. And the Lord tells everyone why: lest Adam and Eve take from it, and eat, and live forever (Gen 3:22–24). God is clearly implying, if not stating outright, that the tree of life is what enabled them to live forever. It had let them overcome their natural, biological boundaries. Blocking access to this tree may be viewed as God's punishment or God's mercy. An indefinite physical life on earth is no tremendous blessing if it is lived under conditions of separation from God, unceasing suffering, and increasing spiritual morbidity.

Based on Old Testament scholarship and Orthodox Christian theology, we have just proposed a paradigm shift—that Adam and Eve were not the first mammals of the human species but the first spiritual people, the first priests, the first to be called by God. They are where the story begins for us. Adam and Eve were mortals who became immortal in relationship to God, not immortals who became mortal in relationship to Satan. Sin is still separation from God, and that separation still results in physical death, but this shift really is a paradigm shift and not just a distinction without a difference.

If Adam and Eve were mortal from the start, it allows for more continuity in the design of biological life. If animals killed and ate each other all along, it explains why the Bible makes no mention of God suddenly reconfiguring appetites and digestive tracts. It isn't mentioned because it never happened. This reading shifts the focus to spiritual transformation. It also, importantly, changes the trajectory of the biblical narrative. We are able to see, through eyes of the heart, a story of mortals gradually ascending, receiving grace upon grace to become like God (2 Pet 1:3) rather than a story of gods who start out at the top, then right away mess up, and just keep messing up. "God knows how we were made; he remembers that we are dust" (Ps 103:14). We might have more compassion for ourselves and others if we too knew and remembered how mortal we are, even from the start.

The preceding reading of Genesis includes some "reading in," which is the case with any interpretation. Genesis has layers of meaning, and the first chapters are especially terse yet evocative. Little wonder that Christians have consulted the New Testament to gain clarity. For example, Revelation spells out that the serpent in the garden was the devil in disguise, as many had suspected all along.

To understand more about Adam and Eve, and more about the connection between sin and death, Christians have turned to the letters of Paul. Do these letters support the reading of Genesis just set forth? I think the answer is yes.

Wait a second. Paul calls Adam "the first man." Is he not saying that Adam was the first person on earth? Paul writes, "As in Adam all die." Is he not saying that all human (and animal) death was punishment for Adam's and Eve's first sin? I think the answer is no, he is not saying these things. But seeing why requires going beyond sound bites.

CHAPTER 23

What Did Paul Actually Say?

A s a starting place, all readers of Paul's epistles can agree he is focused on spiritual patterns more than biological origins.

For example, when Paul says, "Abraham is the father of us all" (Rom 4:16), he does not mean that Abraham is our biological father but rather the spiritual father of all who have Abraham's type of faith. People today hearing the word *father* may think immediately of biological fatherhood, and no doubt most of Paul's audience did too, which is why Paul spells it out: yes, Abraham had many physical offspring, but he is "the father of us all" in a sense that is not physical. He is the father of those "who walk in the footsteps of faith" (Rom 4:12 NIV) and are thus set right with God (Rom 4:3).

If Abraham is this type of father (not biological), then could Adam also be this type of "first man" (not biological)? To answer that question, we need to do a little more work.

Paul says, "Adam was a type of the one to come" (Rom 5:14). This phrase shows that Paul wants his readers to focus on spiritual patterns. We don't need to know Adam's exact hair color or skin tone. We should instead consider Adam in juxtaposition with the "one to come," who is Christ. Whenever Paul mentions Adam, he is talking about Christ in the same breath. Adam's importance lies in comparison with Jesus.

Paul puts this comparison most succinctly in his first letter to the Corinthians, when he says, "The first man was from the earth, a man of dust; the second man is from heaven" (1 Cor 15:47). If our minds were trained in childhood to think that Adam was the first biological human, then we will naturally insert this meaning. But is it the best meaning? Let's see: "The first [biological] man was from the earth, a man of dust; the second [biological] man is from heaven." But the second man, who is from heaven, is obviously Christ, not Cain. Paul is not focused on biology when he says "first" and "second."

To make better sense of this verse, we need to recall that Paul in 1 Corinthians 15 is speaking about types of humans, and more specifically, types of human bodies. People today worry about their various body types and shapes, but for Paul, there are basically just two body types: the mortal dust type and the immortal resurrection type. In saying the first man was from earth and the second man from heaven, Paul is telling the Corinthians that a Christian first has a physical body on earth, then receives a spiritual body at the resurrection. Adam and Christ, as "first" and "second" people, demonstrate these two types of bodies. Adam came from earth and was inherently mortal ("a man of dust"), and he shows the first type of body we have: a physical body that dies. Christ came from heaven, is immortal, and reveals the second type of body we will receive: a spiritual body that is imperishable (1 Cor 15:42).

In short, "first" and "second" in 1 Corinthians 15 do not mean first in history and second in history. They mean first and second types of people, and more specifically, first and second types of bodies. Paul is explaining the resurrection in this passage, and the words *first* and *second* need to be understood in this context.

In this same passage, Paul also refers to Christ as the "last Adam," in contrast to "the first man, Adam" (1 Cor 15:45). Christ being the "last Adam" does not mean he was historically the last person to walk the face of the earth. Likewise, Adam being "the first man" does not have to mean the first person on earth. "First" and "last" in this context mean first in line and last in line. In the project of creating mortals who have an eternal relationship with God, Adam was the first in line. "The first man Adam became a living being" (1 Cor 15:45). As a mortal, he became a living being, for he *received* true life in communion with God. Christ is the last in line, for he not only becomes living but *gives* true life to all who follow; he is himself a "life-giving Spirit" (1 Cor 15:45) who is able to raise mortal bodies from death.

In the context of the letter, therefore, Adam coming before Christ means primarily that the mortal body comes before the resurrection body: first type of body, second type of body; first in line, last in line. These verses are not focused on the earth's population count at the time of Adam and Eve.

We turn to a different question. Even if Paul is not claiming that Adam is the first human being, does he not state outright that Adam and Eve are the cause of all human death? Paul writes, "Sin came into the world through one man, and death came through sin, and so death spread to all, because all have sinned" (Rom 5:12). He also writes, "Many died through the one man's trespass" (Rom 5:15).

Here again, the theory decides what we are able to see. From childhood, many Christians are taught a theory of sin and death that says (a) all people are born sinful (due to "original sin" or to having a "sin nature"), and (b) there was no physical death before Adam and Eve. On this theory, Adam and Eve were made to be physically immortal, but their first trespass changed the structure of their DNA or souls or something essential in them. In an instant, God's original design for humanity became corrupted by human sin, and the defect of sin became passed on to all their descendants. On this view, each and every biological person inherits sin. This sin is why all people die, death being the fitting penalty for sin.

Many find this explanation familiar, and many find it compelling. And many famous people, including Augustine and Aquinas, have contributed to its articulation. But is this explanation the best reading of Romans? I would suggest it is not and would like to offer instead a reading consistent with the idea that God is doing relational creation in Genesis. In this new and ancient reading (which was never lost from view in the Eastern Orthodox tradition), sin is not an innate state that people inherit. Rather, Paul describes sin as a spiritual force that "came into the world" (Rom 5) before he depicts this force invading human flesh (Rom 7). A close reading of Paul does not disallow physical death before Adam and Eve. His discourse on death is open-ended enough for us to view Adam and Eve as mortals who received the hope of immortality and not as immortals who first caused physical mortality.

In looking more closely, let's deal first with the question of sin, then with death. Here are three reasons to think Paul is *not* saying that Adam and Eve caused all people to become born sinners. First, the idea of innate sinfulness runs counter to the overall arc of Paul's argument. In Romans 4 and 5, Paul is talking about the faith of Abraham and the sin of Adam. He says being physically descended from Abraham does not make people faithful. It would be strange, to say the least, if he were suddenly shifting course to claim that being physically descended from Adam *does* make people sinful.

Yes, as a hypothetical, one could propose that biology makes all sinful but none righteous. Yet it's hard to imagine Paul taking this position. His letter argues against the view that spiritual realities are biologically determined. He is explaining to Jews and Gentiles alike that God's covenant with people is based on freedom—God's freedom to call and human freedom to respond. The glorious liberty of God's children (Rom 8:21) is a central node in Romans, and this freedom comes through the Spirit, not biological connections.

A close reading of Paul's words yields a second reason to doubt that all people inherit sin and guilt from Adam and Eve. He says, "All have sinned" (Rom 3:23; 5:12). These words state what people have done, not how they were born. Paul goes on to talk about Adam's sin in comparison with Christ's righteousness, saying, "For just as by the one man's disobedience the many were made sinners, so by the one man's obedience the many will be made righteous" (Rom 5:19). Again, the second half of the comparison sheds light on the first. How does Christ's obedience make many people righteous? They are made righteous not by a biological connection to Jesus, Mary, and Joseph but by a spiritual connection—by being united with Christ spiritually and baptismally and then by following Christ's example as they live out the good works that God prepared in advance for them to do. Christ opens the door and clears the path for righteousness to rule in the world. By contrast, Adam opened the door and cleared the path for sin to come into the world, and many people followed his example of disobedience. Sin and righteousness are primarily spiritual realities caused by spiritual connections, not biological connections.

Since Paul, in his letter to the Romans, never actually says that all people are born sinful, other verses are rallied to shore up this idea. For instance, Ephesians 2:3 says, "We were by nature children of wrath." The word *nature* can sound like something innate, but is it in this case? All the surrounding words and phrases in Ephesians are talking about what people have done to become sinful, not how they were born. To use an analogy: people who have become alcoholics might say they are, by nature, going to drink, but this statement does not mean they were born with vodka in their bloodstream.

Another verse that causes confusion is Psalm 51:5, where the psalmist appears to say that he was "born guilty" or "sinful from birth." But these translations represent interpretations not found in the original manuscripts. A more literal translation of the Masoretic text makes it clear that the psalmist is talking about the condition surrounding his birth, not his innate state: "in sin did my mother conceive me." In Jewish tradition, David was conceived from a relationship of adultery, which would explain this verse (as well as Psalm 69, where he complains that he is a stranger to his own siblings). In Psalm 51:5, the speaker does not say whether the sin surrounding conception was something specific like adultery or a more general condition of being conceived and born into a sinful world. But the psalm at any rate does not support an assertion that people are born with sin infused into their body or soul. This latter idea is found much later in history, particularly in the writings of Augustine.

A third reason to doubt that Paul is proposing people are innately sinful concerns the connection between sin and death. In Paul's mind, this connection is tight: sin inevitably leads to death (Rom 6:23). But Paul's mind was also shaped by studying the prophets, who clearly foretold that God was going to make a covenant in which each person would die for his or her own sins, not for guilt inherited from their parents or grandparents—or, for that matter, from Adam and Eve (Ezek 18:20; Jer 31:30).

To arrive at a better reading of Romans, we need to take off the theoretical glasses that make sin look like a biological condition. For Paul, sin is not hidden somewhere in the strands of human DNA. Sin is instead a spiritual force, and it is not hidden; it is palpably at work in the world. "Sin came into world" (Rom 5:12), says Paul. Sin is out there, not just in the mind. This idea that sin is a force at work in the world goes back to Genesis, where sin is first mentioned. When Cain is enraged and about to kill his brother, the Lord warns him, "Sin is lurking at the door" (Gen 4:7). God does not say, "Remember, Cain, you were born with a sinful nature that you inherited from your parents." Rather, God describes sin as a force, crouching at the door.

Sin causes separation and also enmity between people and God, and between people and people, and even internal warfare between "flesh" and "spirit" within a single person. This definition of sin—as separation from God and opposition to God—is not stated outright, but we can easily infer this meaning by how Paul describes Christ. Paul says Christ died for us when we were sinners (Rom 5:8)—when we were enemies against God (5:10). When we were in this condition, Christ reconciled us to God (5:10–11). If reconciliation is the solution, then the problem must be the opposite of reconciliation—namely, sin-caused separation and sin-filled enmity, animosity, and hostility. Sin began to cause these problems when it came into the world. And there is no doubt that Adam and Eve are the agents who brought sin into the world.

Building on Paul, we can say that Adam and Eve are both the first saints and the first sinners. They are the first to be given the priestly vocation of representing God on earth and the first to rebel against this vocation by seizing and consuming creation apart from God. Their actions change them internally and also unleash a new force of separation, hostility, and violence in the world. The effects are seen right away: sin crouches at the door and pounces on Cain at the moment he is most vulnerable, so he proceeds to murder his brother.

It's time to talk about death. As Paul explains it, the trespass of Adam also brought death along with sin: "Sin came into the world through one man, and death came through sin" (Rom 5:12). Death always carries physical connotations; the murder of Abel was clearly a physical death. But we need to let physical death recede to the background for a moment. We need to take off the physical glasses and put on spiritual lenses to see what is most important to Paul's mind. Like sin, death is also a spiritual force. "Death exercised dominion," says Paul (Rom 5:14). Death is a power at work in the world, and it becomes a condition that plagues people.

Death as a spiritual force starts with Adam, even if physical death was a part of the physical universe that existed before Adam. Strong support for thinking about death in spiritual terms comes in the next chapter of Romans. Paul tells his audience, "We died with Christ" (Rom 6:8) and "We died to sin" (Rom 6:2). Paul is speaking to people who are biologically alive. The death to which he refers is baptismal and spiritual union with Christ. This death is good because it involves dying to the forces that are killing us. Christ's death and our union with him are the solution to the problem of sin and death. If the solution is a good spiritual dying that brings union with God, then we can infer the initial problem was a spiritual death that caused separation from God. In Genesis, God said, "On the day you eat of it you will die." God's word was true: Eve and Adam died—spiritually—on the very day they sinned, even though their biological existence continued for hundreds of years thereafter.

In short, if Paul is saying that Adam is the one who brought spiritual death into the world, then physical death could easily have been a fact of life before Adam and Eve. Physical death, after all, is woven into the order of creation, and it is not always a bad thing. Jesus himself notes that a grain of wheat goes into the ground and dies—in order to bear much fruit, which is a good thing. Physical death is a principle of life and growth in the physical universe. But spiritual death is the result of separation from God and rebellion against God. As such it needs to be defeated, which is what Christ does on the cross. And his victory is ours when we are united with him. This is Paul's line of reasoning in Romans.

Spiritual death and physical death are distinct but also related. The pattern of Chalcedon calls for distinction but also union. Therefore, having separated the spiritual and physical, we now need to unite them. We want to be able to offer young people a coherent narrative that takes into account both Genesis and Romans, both the external and internal forces of sin, and both the spiritual and physical dimensions of death. This coherence will help them read the Bible. It will help them unite faith and science.

Before turning to this task, let's pause to consider the benefit of reading Romans through spiritual eyes of the heart—specifically, the benefit of seeing sin and death as spiritual forces rather than focusing on sin as an innate, quasi-biological condition. The benefit becomes clearer when we ask the following questions: How do we teach young people about sin in a way that is life-giving? And how do we teach about sin in a society where sin has become passé?

In seminary, I took a class on Romans and the theology of Paul. Our professor had been imprisoned in a Nazi concentration camp when he was a teenager. Paul wrote about sin as a force at work in the world, and in that concentration camp our professor saw what Paul meant. He witnessed the power of sin firsthand. But when he taught us in later years, he wondered aloud whether Paul's message would hit home for young people today. "There are a lot of happy sinners in this country," he used to say, his voiced tinged with irony. Sin is not part of our public discourse, in part because public knowledge is provided by scientists and social scientists, whose theories and instruments are not designed to detect sin.

In response, people in youth ministry feel torn. For some youth workers, sin is the first thing they want to talk about with young people; for others, it is the last. But neither group is completely happy. Those who teach on sin and salvation wonder how to do so in a way that does not manipulate youthful emotions or recapitulate oppressive feelings of guilt and shame they themselves were made to feel growing up. Those who omit talk of sin may feel uneasy about neglecting a major theme of Christian Scripture and tradition.

The problem then becomes figuring out the right portion of shame and guilt. Shame is toxic, but to be shameless is also not good. Guilt is oppressive, but having no conscience is worse. This problem is interesting, but it is the wrong starting place for viewing sin, and it comes from looking in the wrong direction. Sin is a power in the world before it becomes an internal condition issuing in feelings of shame, guilt, or remorse. The snake is lurking in the garden before Adam and Eve eat forbidden fruit. To teach well on sin, therefore, means talking about evil and even Satan, not obsessively or with undue fascination but as a matter-of-fact description of the spiritual universe.

A glimpse into this spiritual universe comes from Scott Peck, author and psychologist, who describes counseling Bobby, a depressed and despondent teenager. Bobby's older brother had recently committed suicide. During a session shortly after Christmas one year, the psychologist asks the adolescent what gifts he received. "Nothing much," Bobby replies. The conversation continues:

> "Your parents must have given you something. What did they give you?"
>
> "A gun."
>
> "A gun?" I repeated stupidly.
>
> "Yes."
>
> "What kind of gun?" I asked slowly.
>
> "A twenty-two."
>
> "A twenty-two pistol."
>
> "No, a twenty-two rifle."
>
> There was a long moment of silence. . . . Finally I pushed myself to say what had to be said. "I understand it was with a twenty-two rifle that your brother killed himself."
>
> "Yes."
>
> "Was that what you asked for for Christmas?"
>
> "No."
>
> "What did you ask for?"
>
> "A tennis racket."
>
> "But you got a gun instead?"
>
> "Yes."

"How did you feel, getting the same kind of gun that your brother had?"

"It wasn't the same kind of gun."

I began to feel better. Maybe I was just confused. "I'm sorry," I said. "I thought they were the same kind of gun."

"It wasn't the same kind of gun," Bobby replied. "It was the gun."

"The gun?"

"Yes."

"You mean it was your brother's gun?" I wanted to go home very badly now.

"Yes."

"You mean your parents gave you your brother's gun for Christmas, the one he shot himself with?"

"Yes."[1]

This is when Peck, as a human scientist, realized he was dealing with the presence of evil. Not just evil as the privation or absence of goodness but evil as a force whose palpable presence was crouching at the door of the room where he sat.

This account is not meant to make us more fearful when working with young people but more aware. Extreme manifestations of good and evil point to a more generalized condition that does not always rise to the level of consciousness. If we are sometime forced to feel the presence of evil, then we are also free to feel, palpably, the presence of God. The Bible talks extensively about spiritual forces of good and evil, but the church today seems less adept with this language, prone either to a despiritualizing dismissal that says it's all in our head or to the opposite error, an over-spiritualizing that pictures demons behind every bush.

Good teaching on sin is part of the gospel. For a young person, it is good news to know the problem I face is not simply a lack of willpower or a personal failure to do good deeds. The problem of sin is bigger than I am,

[1] M. Scott Peck, *People of the Lie: The Hope for Healing Human Evil* (New York: Simon and Schuster, 1983), 51–52.

and so too is the solution. A worldview with large and looming spiritual forces still has plenty of room for personal responsibility. We are responsible for how we deal with what we are dealt. The goal of teaching on this topic is to foster a balanced, realistic perspective, spiritually speaking.

So far, we have tried to take the focus off biology in Genesis and Romans. We are considering the proposal that sin and death are forces at work in the world, which work in tandem. This proposal also says biological death was part of God's original design for this present physical universe. An encounter with the spiritual force of sin and death always pushes Paul closer to Christ, as it should us too. To support this progress toward intimacy with God, let's try to explain, in words that can easily be understood, what is going on in Genesis and Romans. Having taken the focus off biology, let's look again, through eyes of the heart, at what these portions of the Bible tell us about death and life.

The Gospel, Part I: "In the Beginning"

The gospel can be presented to youth in more ways than one. As two primary ways, we can talk about sin and salvation, or we can talk about death and life. It has been said that Christianity in the West has tended to stress the good news of forgiveness for sin, while over the centuries, the East placed more emphasis on victory over death.

In an age of science, the latter approach may be the more effective. People who doubt they are sinners still know they are going to die. The ratio of one death per person has remained fairly constant and is still a compelling statistic. Death gets our attention like nothing else, and in this respect, it has been called one of our best teachers. Though people labor mightily to repress the thought of dying, and though some, like Darwin, will avoid going to funerals, nevertheless death will always erupt on the scene sooner or later.

Drawing together strands from prior chapters, the goal now is to show, in terms a teenager can grasp, why the death of Christ is central to the gospel. We will not jump right away to the resurrection, since resurrections are less empirically observable than deaths. Rather, we will want to talk first about the life of Jesus. If youth understand his life, they will be able to understand his death. And if they grasp his death, they will be able to see why his resurrection was not impossible but inevitable. Paul says, "death no longer has dominion over him" (Rom 6:9). Death has lost its dominion over Jesus and by extension lost its authority to rule over the person who is joined to Jesus. Christ liberates people from death's dominion. To convey this Easter message, we need to explain how the power of life in Christ overcomes the power of death in the world.

The discussion of life could start in Genesis, or we could jump right away to John's prologue, which says of Jesus, "In him was life." Since we have been talking about Genesis, let's start there, though this tack will take longer. (When actually speaking with youth, we can space it out.) And since we have been talking about science, let's start with a scientific term.

Scientists sometimes speak of the current age as the Anthropocene period, by which they mean humans (*anthropoi*, in Greek) have become a dominant influence on the environment. Scientists differ on when exactly the Anthropocene age began. Some give it a recent date, when human effects on the environment have been most obvious.

If the Anthropocene period entails a significant human impact on the environment, then in biblical and archetypal terms, it starts in the Garden. If we want to understand ecologic problems or economic problems—or really any human problem at all—spiritually, then we must begin with humanity's relationship to God. How we relate to God affects all other relationships. So we start with Adam and Eve.

We begin there, because that is where the story begins for us. The universe is replete with untold stories. Astrophysicists report life-forms are probably living on other planets today; they expect to find liquid water and other evidence in the near future. The Bible does not discuss how God would relate to these other life-forms. Likewise, archaeologists tell us that biological humans have been on the scene for some time, well before the times of Genesis. The Bible does not discuss how God related to those other people. We can ponder such questions another day, using biblical and theological clues, but for now, the goal is to understand the Christian story that starts with Adam and Eve.

Starting with them does not mean trying to dig up their bones. Whatever their historical status, and whether or not we are related biologically to people like Adam and Eve or Abraham and Sarah, these people are spiritual ancestors for all Christians. Exactly when they lived is less important than why. Adam and Eve represent the first people whom God calls.

God creates people, places, and things by calling them to be in relationship with God. True life consists in relationality with God. This understanding of creation does not contradict the Christian teaching that God created the entire universe out of nothing—*ex nihilo*. The doctrine of creation *ex nihilo* reminds us that God always existed, before anything physical. Go back as far as you can think, before any material molecules, and still there was God. God always was and is and will be.

How material molecules came to exist and how God brought something out of nothing are valid questions but not the questions Genesis addresses. In Genesis, God is working with material molecules that already exist. What is God doing? Some people read Genesis as the account of God shaping material molecules into physical form. But the ancient Hebrews would not have read Genesis this way, nor is it the best reading for us today. Genesis is not offering a theory in competition with the big bang or neo-Darwinian evolution. Those scientific theories, in all their complexity, must stand or fall on scientific evidence. But Genesis is telling us why all the material stuff really matters, which science does not discuss.

Physical matter matters because God is creating the cosmos to be a home. Even the famous scientist Stephen Hawking once said it would not be much of a universe unless it were home to the people we love. How a universe becomes a home is not a scientific process; it is a spiritual process. This is what Genesis depicts, with particular focus on one planet. God's Spirit is moving over the face of the waters to create spiritual order. God's voice is speaking and giving everything its meaning, purpose, and power to exist in relation to God. In the world of the Bible, a thing or person does not truly exist or have life apart from God.

God is creating the earth to be a particular kind of home called a temple. In the world of the Bible, the temple is the place from which God rules:

The Lord is in his holy temple;
the Lord is on his heavenly throne. (Ps 11:4, NIV)

The psalm may be talking about a temple in Jerusalem, but Genesis depicts the whole earth as becoming God's temple and throne room. Though a small planet, Earth makes for a large temple, humanly speaking. And humans do speak; humans have a crucial part to play. Here is where Adam and Eve come in. They are the first priests in this temple called Earth. They are the first king and queen of God's kingdom.

In the ancient Near East, as we noted earlier, kings alone were said to be the gods' representatives. Kings possessed the image and/or likeness of gods; they alone had this power and dominion. But Genesis tells a different story, which is pertinent to young people coming to a sense of their identity and wondering about their worth. Adam and Eve (whose names mean Man and Living) reveal that all people are created to share in God's image and likeness. While Adam and Eve are the first priests and royals, they are also not alone. The people of Israel are called to be a "royal priesthood," and in the New Testament, this calling is extended to the church.

People living in the United States may have a love-hate relationship with the idea of European royalty, but probably everyone likes to think of being in charge—say, when planting a field, writing software, or making a painting. We all desire royal power in one sphere or another. What kind of royals are we going to be? Royalty entails responsibility. Humans have a lot of power, for good or ill, and whether we realize it or not. Someone may say, "I just want to do me." That's fine, but I need to keep in mind that what I do affects other people and even the entire earth.

Adam and Eve were never meant to go it alone; they were meant to be priests and royals in relation to God. As royals, our human calling or vocation is to care for the earth and to be its benefactor. We are to use our God-given powers to love and protect. Royals receive creation from God. Priests offer creation back to God. We are called to be both and to do both. What is offered to God becomes sacred. Priests then consume what is sacred—taking creation into our minds and bodies, in relationship to God, as a means of communing with God and of sharing with others.

But Adam and Eve become consumers in a more modern sense of the word. They take and consume creation to satisfy their own desire. To be sure, human desires can also be God given. God implants desires in our heart, and the fulfillment of these desires draws us closer to God. There is, however, one kind of desire that separates us from God, and this is the desire with which the tempter tempted them.

The desire that causes separation from God is the desire to be like God apart from God. God had created Adam and Eve to be like God in communion with God. But the serpent said they didn't need God to be like God: "For God knows that when you eat the fruit you will become like God"—all on your own. The serpent lied. As priests and royals, Adam and Eve learn about evil by doing evil, and in the process invite sin to rule in the world.

We don't need to know the exact taste or texture of the fruit they ate. We are looking through spiritual eyes at the godlike powers entrusted to us. Humans can invent vaccines to cure disease or germ warfare to spread disease. In communion with God, we can do all kinds of good; separated from God, all manner of evil.

We can step back now and see why the world needs Jesus. We are dealing with problems of sin and death, and these problems are too big to handle on our own. Sin is a small word that denotes the big problem of separation from God. Sin can refer to physical deeds that people do, but sin is also a spiritual power that came into the world.

Death is likewise both physical and spiritual. Physical death is a normal and natural part of the physical universe. A grain of wheat goes into the ground and dies so that more abundant fruit can grow. Spiritual death, however, is the outgrowth of sin, and like sin, it spells separation from God.

How, then, are we to view physical death? On the one hand, we know it is normal, expected, and inescapable. On the other hand, for humans, physical death means we have fallen short of our calling. We are meant to live forever, in communion with God. That is what it means to be fully and truly human. In creating people, God transforms mortals into immortals. Adam and Eve were given the tree of life, which is death's antidote—the medicine of immortality.

So yes, death is still physically normal and natural. It is also normal and natural for many organisms to kill and eat their young, but not for humans to do so. And likewise, for humans who have been called into an eternal relationship with God, death now becomes abnormal, unnatural, and truly horrible. We rightly rebel against death because physical death has become for us the result of spiritual death. Our hearts are not meant to bear eternal separation from the people we love; our minds are not supposed to tolerate the thought of total nonexistence.

This is precisely where Jesus comes in—as the defeater of death and giver of life.

CHAPTER 25

The Gospel, Part II: "Death, Thou Shalt Die"

Death makes life feel limited rather than abundant. Death makes us fearful and anxious by telling us we have a finite time to fulfill our infinite desire. Fear of death, says the writer of Hebrews, is what the devil uses to keep people in bondage (Heb 2:15).

Death can drive people to desperation. Priests consume creation as a means of communion with God, but fallen priests, driven by death, try to turn creation, other people, and even God into a means of satisfying their self-centered desires. Royals use their creative powers for God-given purposes, but fallen royals, driven by death, put those powers to ignoble use.

Yet faith affirms that the life of God coursing through us is still greater than the power of death in the world. This life is not some impersonal energy in the universe—for the physical universe is slowly dying too—but rather, this life comes to us in the person of Jesus, God in flesh. John's Gospel says of Jesus, "In him was life" (John 1:4). This life, in all its fullness, is apprehended through spiritual eyes of the heart. Physically speaking, after all, Jesus was nothing special to behold (Isa 51:2). The world observes a man who survived for about thirty-three years, then was tortured to death. The physical description is accurate but far from adequate to sum up or contain the life that is in Jesus. Even the physical grave cannot contain his life.

People sense life is more than physical. People who are not believers or especially spiritual may say, "I don't want merely to exist; I want to be truly alive!" Here they imply life is a quality of being more than a quantity of time. This life is what Jesus lived from the start. "In him was life, and the life was the light of all people" (John 1:4). Everywhere he goes, Jesus shines light. Everyone he touches, he heals. Everything he encounters, he transforms—including death.

From the start, powers of evil were arrayed against him. Jesus was born a king and destined to restore people to their true royalty, which meant using his God-given power to redeem the world. But a fallen king named Herod tried to kill Jesus. Jesus escaped; however, babies and infants were murdered by the fallen king and became the first martyrs.

When he was about thirty years old, Jesus was anointed with the Spirit. He became a priest in the fullest sense—bringing God's gifts to the people and offering himself as humanity's perfect gift to God. This offering was complete: the sacrifice of his life. Fallen priests conspired against Jesus, the Roman Empire got involved, and in the end, the whole world stood convicted of the crime of killing the Son of God. But Jesus told them he did not come to condemn the world. He came to condemn death and the power of death at work in the world.

The crucifixion of Jesus had both physical agony and spiritual vitality. "For the joy set before him, he endured the cross" (Heb 12:2 NIV). His dying was not his life's end but rather its fullest expression. Every impulse, every breath, including his dying breath, consisted of love for God and love for people. He prayed, "Father, forgive them." Jesus was never more alive than at the hour of his death.

Life this full and powerful is able to fill even death. For what is death? It is separation from God. It is separation from people we love, from the world, from ourselves. But Jesus, in his death, overcame this separation. This death, his death, was not separation from God but an act of obedience to God and union with God, for he went to the cross in free and full agreement with the Father's will. He took the separation and forsakenness of death ("My God, my God, why have you forsaken me?") into himself and undid it. This death, his death, was not separation from the world and its people, for he died to redeem the world and reconcile people.

Therefore, in his dying, Jesus transformed death. In fact, death itself died and gave rise to fuller life. This new reality is seen through eyes of the heart. Adam and Eve transformed physical death into spiritual death when they fell short of their calling to become like God. But Christ transformed physical death into fuller life by removing death's sting. As Alexander Schmemann says, he makes death a "passover" to closer union with God.

There is no doubt Jesus was crucified, died, and was buried. With their own eyes, people saw him die, and it looks impossible for a person so completely dead to rise again. But no, says Peter. "It was impossible for death to keep its hold on him!" (Acts 2:24 NIV). "In him was life"—too much life to be held in death's grip. The power of death is too weak, the power of Christ's life too great. He must come bursting forth.

To recap, his life led inescapably to his death, given the evil that is in the world. But his death led inevitably to his resurrection, given the life of God in him. Further, this resurrection is not his alone. Matthew gives the astonishing report that when Jesus rose from the grave, many other people also came out of their tombs and were seen walking about Jerusalem. Resurrection became a communal event, and this story gives us a preview of what awaits the whole creation, as it groans for its final culmination.

Here is where faith comes in. We still see physical death as part of the natural world and a fact of human life. But faith looks forward to a day when the entire world reaches spiritual fulfillment and when people are finally and fully liberated, even from the bondage of physical death. In the meantime, we have work to do—the work that comes as a result of Jesus having restored humanity to our rightful place as royal priests. By his Spirit, we have power to transform the world once again into a communion with God; to love the people God places in our path; to care for people who are hungry, naked, or imprisoned, because these people are like Jesus in disguise (Matt 25:31–48).

In doing this work, we inevitably witness and experience suffering. For many people, suffering is harder than death. An old-time Pentecostal pastor wrote, "Praying for the sick was a significant part of our ministry and we believed we must pray for them until they either recovered or died. We didn't think dying was terrible; we only thought suffering was terrible. . . . We prayed, 'Lord, if you don't intend to heal them, take them home.' And we prayed them well or dead."[1]

Suffering raises more questions than anyone can answer this side of eternity. But the topic is sure to arise with young people. In contemplating the cross of Jesus and "the joy set before him" (Heb 12:2 NIV), we can say a couple of things. First, suffering is not always without purpose, and hopefully it is never without hope. If we can endure, it will end, and for some (for all eventually), physical death provides release from suffering.

Second, people are not meant to endure alone. We are called to accompany each other through terrible physical pain and chasms of emotional despair. As royal priests, we are meant to bring God's presence to the world, which means being truly present to one another. The priestly example of Christ leads us to love as he did, freely and sacrificially. Today this love must include the sacrifice of our precious time, which is no small thing. At least then we can alleviate the horrible loneliness and isolation that so often make suffering unbearable.

We recall young Charles Darwin, whose faith became shipwrecked on rocks that were at once intellectual, emotional, and deeply personal. The preceding presentation of the gospel could go a long way toward helping a young Charles Darwin make peace between his Christian faith and scientific pursuits. These words could help him see that biological death and spiritual death are different but related, just as the insights of science and faith are distinct but ultimately able to be unified.

Yet what could possibly have helped Darwin deal with the death of his daughter? There is a time to speak, but our ministry needs to be more than words. There are times when what matters most is being there,

---

[1] David du Plessis, as told to Bob Slosser, *A Man Called Mr. Pentecost* (Plainfield, NJ: Logos International, 1977), 29.

present to the person who suffers, open to the presence of God. Real presence, like life itself, is not merely a physical occupation of the same space but a spiritual quality that sustains hope. It involves indwelling the space between yourself and the one who is suffering, even inbreathing it with the presence of Christ, who makes it sacred.

CHAPTER 26

But Why?

The preceding telling of the gospel raises questions about an area of theology called atonement, which the next two chapters aim to address. Many books have been written on this topic. My purpose is not to redo the work of better scholars or undo the beliefs of better Christians but rather to shed light on a central theme of this book. Seeing through eyes of the heart means thinking relationally. Relational creation in Genesis is just the beginning. Thinking relationally gives us insight into all of reality, including the cross that stands at the center of Christian history.

"But why did Jesus have to die?" asked my son Andrew, age three, as he was sitting up from a nap. His tone sounded detached, philosophical. He had recently learned about Jesus's death from a video.

I paused. The question caught me off guard. Then I said, "That's what Mommy is going to teach you about later." To be fair to me, it wasn't clear whether he was asking a direct question or pondering aloud.

In either case, the naked simplicity of a toddler's question reveals why we like simple, natural, scientifically verifiable answers. They seem to put us on safer ground. My mind, before going blank, ran through some of these empirical-sounding answers. Everyone has to die, sooner or later—biologically true but beside the point, since his question concerned Jesus in particular. Jesus did not want to die. He loved people and tried to help them in every way. But bad people got together and killed him.

This answer, also true, was vacant of theological content. In the Gospels, Jesus clearly sees his death as being God's will. This is what I wanted to be able to explain to my three-year-old. But how? Should I tell him that Jesus died to appease God's wrath (Isa 53:5) or to demonstrate God's love (Rom 5:8)?

Obviously, a toddler is unable to grasp concepts we might convey to a teenager, but now and then, it is good to test our theology at the toddler level. If we can simplify our ideas without undue distortion, for any age level, then we have accomplished a central task of teaching. The complementary task is being able to illuminate complex facets of simple-sounding statements, such as $E = mc^2$ or "God is love."

As it turned out, the children's video that prompted my son's question also supplied the answer, or at least an answer. When I asked him later, "Andrew, why did Jesus have to die?" he smiled and replied, "Jesus died so that we can choose to be friends with God." Now it was my turn to ponder.

On reflection, I decided this was a pretty good answer. It stressed the biblical idea of reconciliation, putting it in the language of friendship, also biblical and fitting for a three-year-old. The answer left ample room for parents and pastors to fill in details over time. How exactly did the death of Christ open the door to our friendship with God? Did it change God's judgment of us or our understanding of God? Parents could teach as they saw fit. In terms of the atonement typology of Gustaf Aulén, they could take the path of either Anselm's "satisfaction" theory or Abelard's "moral exemplar" theory.[1]

"Jesus died so that we can choose . . ." I noted with approval an emphasis on human decision in the reconciliation process, even if, as I also believed, the grace that draws us toward this decision is nearly irresistible.

The answer my son has learned is at root a sin-and-salvation message. Without erasing a word of it, I will want him also to learn the good news discussed in prior chapters, which is a message of life and death. Summed

---

[1] Gustaf Aulén, *Christus Victor: An Historical Study of the Three Main Ideas of the Atonement*, trans. A. G. Herbert (London: SPCK, 1970).

up in the Paschal *troparion* (Easter song) of the Eastern Orthodox Church, it says:

Christ is risen from dead,
trampling down death by death,
and upon those in the tombs bestowing life.

Translated into a child's language: Jesus died so that we can live together forever with God.

In terms of Aulén's typology, this answer corresponds to the *Christus victor* understanding of atonement, which was favored by Irenaeus and subsequent patristic theologians. All three views of Christ's death—he died for our sins; he died to show God's love; he died to defeat sin, death, and the devil—have supporting verses of Scripture. Explaining the atonement may require multiple theories, and even then we may conclude the cross is a mystery that exceeds all explanation.

However, "mystery" should not be an excuse to avoid explaining as much as we can (most *mysteria* in the New Testament are *solved* mysteries—things formerly hidden but now revealed and understood), so I must be prepared for a favorite follow-up question of most children: But why? It's good that God wants to defeat death, but why does Jesus need to die to accomplish this feat? With a snap of the fingers, God could uproot death and replant the tree of life. Why doesn't God do it that way? Finger snapping is often the method people prefer God would use for many problems.

In reply, we need to see three things. First, God's goal is not merely to defeat death, as big as that sounds. Rather, God's goal of defeating death—by transforming it into a passover to fuller life—is part of God's even larger project of transforming all creation. The highlight of God's project is to make people more fully human, according to the humanity revealed in Jesus, and thus make people more like God.

Second, physical death is useful in this project of human transformation. Like almost nothing else, death can get our attention and turn it toward God. Theologian James Loder used to say that God takes death both less seriously and more seriously than we do. What feels so incredibly serious to us is the aching chasm between here and hereafter; the total separation from the whole world and only world we know; the sense that when we die, we must say good-bye finally and forever to all the people we love. God, being God, recognizes that these human feelings are profound; but God, being on both sides of the chasm, sees they are mistaken. The distance between here and hereafter is not as wide as it seems. The separation will be temporary; the reconciliation and joyful reunion will endure forever, in dimensions beyond time. The "finality" of death is what God takes less seriously than we do.

But what God takes more seriously is the capacity of death to teach us how to live well, by focusing our lifetime's energy on what matters most. Many of us have had these moments of clarity after the loss of a loved one. We say to ourselves, "I never want to worry about x again. I'm going to devote much more energy to y. Life is too short to do otherwise."

In T. S. Eliot's poem "Ash Wednesday," the speaker says, "Teach us to care and not to care / Teach us to sit still." Death helps us to care more about what's important and not to care so much about the many things that loom large only because we forget how small they become once we die.

There is a reason parents of former centuries taught their children to meditate on death from an early age. Today we consider it morbid: "If I should die before I wake, I pray the Lord my soul to take." I have yet to share this bedtime prayer with my son. I want him to grow up happy. But part of me does worry whether he will grow up wise. At any rate, God takes more seriously than we do death's pedagogical value. The anticipation of physical death can help us make better use of our earthly time (better does not always mean busier), and then, to stretch the teaching metaphor, the actual experience of physical death becomes our final exam and graduation rolled into one.

If you agree with what was just said, then you can see a vital difference between spiritual death and physical death. Spiritual death, or separation from God, is immediately and always an enemy to be defeated as quickly as possible. Physical death is ultimately an enemy to be defeated ("the last enemy to destroyed is death"; 1 Cor 15:26), but in the near term, it is useful to God's purposes. It is, as we noted, a principle of life and growth in the physical universe, and it is one of God's best teaching assistants. Here we are trying to make sense of the fundamental fact of death, not justify all the circumstances and sufferings of a particular person's death.

A third and most basic reason God transforms death through Jesus, rather than through finger snapping, is this: how God acts always comes from who God is. God's Being is consistently, reliably relational. Relationality starts within the Trinity; it progresses to the relational creation God does in Genesis; and it culminates in the incarnation, whereby God relates to creation deeply and intimately by becoming one of us.

This relationality is reciprocal. The way God in Jesus relates to us is also how we are meant to relate to God—deeply and intimately. He pitches his tent in our neighborhood and abides with us (John 1); we in turn are invited to abide in him (John 15). He is born of our flesh so we can become reborn of his Spirit. He participates fully in our life so that we can participate fully in the life of God. This participation includes death, which is at once the most widely universal and the most deeply personal human experience. By filling the utter agony of death with himself, Christ transforms death into fuller life. This victory becomes ours when we are joined to Jesus. He dies so that we, dying with him, can live forever.

These sayings may be familiar. They are worthy of acceptance, and they have been accepted by many Christians. But for most of us, they belong too exclusively to the Sunday world of faith. How does mental assent begin to feel as real as the pavement or grass under our feet? The new creation God does in Christ, including the transformation of death, has both cosmic and personal consequences. But it is hard to wrap our lives around them because daily reality feels so different.

Though people speak frequently of networks and relationships, all this talk does not mean we have really grasped relational creation. Networks often refer to business transactions, and relationships to individual personal fulfillment. An individual is more apt to say, "I have a relationship," than to think, "I am a relationship." For all our talk of global connectivity, reality for us is less like a pond in which each stone's ripple disturbs the whole and more like a pool table on which balls stand in static isolation unless directly struck by some other ball. We most often perceive ourselves as being autonomous individuals. We are usually buffered from one another and the world around us.

Yet every notion of atonement that actually means what the word says—"at-one-ment"—hinges on the premise that one person can exist in and through another. Whether we are speaking of Christ taking our place on the cross or of our being united with him in his victorious death, the basic idea is that my existence is best defined not by myself or by any inner desire that I feel is authentic to me but by a Person who lived two thousand years before I was physically born. And this idea is what sounds preposterous to all nonbelievers and probably secretly does to many believers.

As evidence of the latter fact, note how prone present-day preachers are to elide the language of the New Testament when talking about baptism and Communion. Baptism, which Paul calls a union with Christ in his death, becomes a rite of passage to join the church or an individual's public profession of faith. Communion, which Paul calls a participation in the blood of Christ, becomes a reminder or "symbol" to aid personal contemplation.

How can I help my son to think relationally when so many cultural messages will be teaching him to think individually? I'm glad he is learning to think of Jesus as his friend; in time, there will be much more along these lines for him—and me—to learn. If Christians can reclaim the sense of relational creation in Genesis and relational new creation in John, it will help us understand atonement better and pave the way to thinking more relationally today.

But thinking this way is hard. When was the last time I said to myself, "I *am* a relationship?"

CHAPTER 27

Atonement Issues

One reason it's hard to see relational creation in Genesis or to think relationally about the atonement is that we have a hard time, in general, thinking this way. Have we become isolated individuals who perceive a world of isolatable entities around us? If so, then some scholars think technology and science are partly to blame.

Technology has given us more mobility to uproot ourselves, to leave our village behind, and even to ensconce ourselves within private digital domes. Science, meanwhile, has shaped our overall sense of reality. The physics of the Enlightenment period (Isaac Newton et al.) depicted a universe of discrete, individual bodies at the same time Enlightenment political science (John Locke et al.) envisioned a society of separate, individual people.

But today's science paints a different picture. The pond rather than the pool table is actually the more accurate depiction of the physical universe. Our sense of separateness and individuality is largely an illusion, even as the wall of solid granite is mainly empty space. In the biosphere, the proverbial flap of the butterfly's wings reminds us that each tiny action affects the whole. At the subatomic level, quantum entanglement—what Einstein (somewhat derisively) called "spooky action at a distance"— means that photons and electrons affect each other even when separated by twelve hundred kilometers of physical space.[1] In short, everything is interconnected, more than we can imagine and in ways we have yet to fathom. We humans are also connected to the whole. In theology, the physical mysticism of Sallie McFague often focuses on our interconnection with the rest of the creation through the air we breathe, water we drink, and food we eat.

If there is one area of theology where we ought to be thinking relationally, it is the death of Jesus, yet so much contemporary teaching either avoids the cross entirely or else turns it into a transaction that sounds oddly legal and businesslike. The latter message is sometimes given by preachers who, in the next breath, will stress that God wants a loving, not a legal, relationship with us. It is almost as if the cross is a nasty piece of legal business that must be gotten out the way in order for the loving relationship to commence. But that is certainly not how Jesus speaks of his own death.

Different Christians face different obstacles to thinking relationally about the atonement. For some, who may call themselves progressive, the challenge is sensing that this relationality is as intimate and personal as two people in a garden walking with God in the cool of the evening—a vivid first picture of relational creation. For others, who may call themselves evangelical, the challenge is seeing that this relationality has cosmic consequences. If a personal relationship with Jesus pulls us out of the world, then it should also fire us back into the world with a greater velocity to love people and care for creation, to work for the peace of the city and healing of the nations—a vivid final picture of relational creation. (Traditional monastics, physically removed from the world, were still actively involved in the world via their prayers of intercession.) Let's try to address these two challenges, first the "progressive" and then the "evangelical."

Many progressive parents want to counteract a version of substitutionary atonement they were taught growing up. Their experience shows

---

[1] Gabriel Popkin, "Spooky Action Achieved at Record Distance," *Science* 356, no. 6343 (June 16, 2017): 1110–11.

how the most common Western teaching of atonement—that Jesus died for our sins by taking our place on the cross—is also the hardest for the modern Western rational mind to grasp. Stated in terms that seem to make the most sense to our minds, it becomes nonsense: I do bad things, so God kills Jesus instead, and that somehow makes it right. Well, if you put it that way, who would want to teach their toddler or teenager this "good news"?

Feeling assured of our more enlightened modern vantage point, and pointing to recent social justice movements as evidence of this fact, we may take a different tack. We may decide to teach a more human-centered view of why Christ died: Jesus was the supreme social justice warrior who stood against the evils of oppression; in the end, these evil forces killed him, but the resurrection (or stories of resurrection) offer hope that justice will one day prevail. In structure, this story is a *Christus victor* narrative, and it is good so far as it goes. But as a total account of atonement, there are at least three reasons it does not go far enough.

First, though a *Christus victor* narrative, it is divested of Christ's real presence and present-day power. The New Testament everywhere speaks of believers living "in Christ," but in this account, Jesus lived two thousand years ago, and we become followers trying to live like Jesus under our own steam.

Second, this account invests all hope in resurrection and none at all in the cross itself. In no sense in this narrative is Good Friday actually good. In an age of science, where seeing is believing, people see a lot of death. Thus it will be an incalculable benefit if we can transform Christ's death itself into good news and not have everything hinge on a resurrection that occurs at the last day. When Martha is focused on this future day, Jesus tells her, "I am [here and now] the resurrection and the life" (John 11:25). Hidden in this statement is the insight that his death already makes inevitable his resurrection; his crucifixion is also his coronation.

Third, the narrative avoids rather than faces the problem of guilt and punishment. We may say this is a good thing. We may point out that too much preaching has been fixated on punishment, and we may point to biblical passages where sacrifice is nowhere in view. When Jesus speaks of his death in John 3, he chooses an image of healing. "As Moses lifted up the serpent in the wilderness, so the Son of Man must be lifted up" (John 3:14): just as the bronze serpent in the wilderness, when looked upon in faith, drew out the snakes' venom, so Jesus intends to draw out the poison in us.

At the same time, we can hardly avoid the motif of sin and sacrifice. We find it plainly in Scripture (e.g., 2 Cor 5:21, where Jesus is called a sin offering), and we discover it deep within our psyches. Consider for a moment victims of rape, torture, or genocide. Should we tell them to silence the "primitive" voice within that says someone must pay? Should we insist the more loving path is simply to forgive and forget, to let bygones be bygones—and by extension assume a loving God would think likewise? When the matter is put in such stark terms, we see that a solution to sin cannot be truly loving unless it is also somehow deeply just.

God does not stand aloof from this problem. The deep justice of God means that God is both the injured party and the One who in Christ suffers sin's consequence. God's redemption of the world is just as relational as God's creation of the world. Here is where my modern rational thinking recoils. When one human individual harms another individual, how can God possibly be the injured party? This question shows how little I actually believe in God or how far removed I think God must be from human affairs. We would not dare tell parents of a harmed child, "You have no right to be upset, since you were not the injured party." Relational creation in Genesis means that God is as close to us as a parent, even before we come to the "Abba" prayers of Jesus. "Image and likeness" is, as we said, a term for kings but also for sons and daughters. Adam's son Seth bears his image and likeness (Gen 5:3). The horror of killing another person, Genesis goes on to say, stems from the fact that people bear God's image (Gen 9:6). When people harm each other, God is indeed an injured party; as the Author of Life, God is the ultimate injured party: "Against you, you alone, have I sinned" (Ps 51:4), says David.

Next, my thinking may recoil in another direction. How can Jesus possibly take responsibility for the offenses of people so far removed from him in space and time? Here again I must face my lost intuition of relational reality. The New Testament declares not only that Jesus died for us but also that we died with him. It speaks of believers living in Jesus, even as Jesus lives in God and God lives in him. But it is very hard for us, as believers, actually to believe these words in the sense of having a strong feeling and intuition for the reality they depict. I am my own person; how can my life possibly be hidden inside someone else (Col 3:3)? In our present age, this idea feels too ethereal, unless made concretely physical, such as an unborn baby existing inside its mother.

Therefore, many Christians either rule out the idea of spiritual union or relegate it to a select few, the "mystics" such as Paul or Julian of Norwich or Teresa of Ávila. Spiritual union is seen as an optional addition to the tour package rather than the main destination printed on the ticket. No doubt the mystics experience this union most intensely. But the basic relational identity—I am joined with Jesus; I have, as Paul says, been crucified with him; I abide, as Jesus says, in him—is probably the basic definition of a Christian.

The thrust of substitutionary atonement thus needs to be relational, not transactional. Sermons that portray atonement as an impersonal business operation, such as payment for sin being transferred from Christ's bank account to ours, tragically lose sight of the fact that God's ultimate purpose in atonement is not avenging sin but transforming sinners.

I am not trying, in the preceding paragraphs, to deal with every objection that progressive Christians might level against traditional atonement doctrines. I simply want to suggest that these problems are metaphysical before they are moral. At root is the question of how we see ourselves in relation to God. When the New Testament applies the language and imagery of Yom Kippur to Jesus, it depicts intimate relationality. The priest placing his hands on the head of the sacrificial animal was establishing a connection largely lost to our modern sensibility.

In general, we all tend to put our theology into terms that make sense to our own culture, and no culture is perfect. In former cultures, it would be easier for me to feel my personhood was conjoined with Jesus and interconnected with the body of Christ but perhaps also too easy to adopt a tribal mentality that squelches individuality and even subjugates entire classes of people. Today, it is easier to honor the particularity of each person and to recognize, via the incarnation, the infinite worth of each individual, but it is harder, as an individual, to feel a communal identity or to feel, as Paul did, that self-fulfillment comes through self-surrender to the One who knows better than I do what it means for me to be me.

The benefit of cross-cultural comparison is that it helps us see our blind spots as well as our better insights. We may see better than they that intimacy with Christ and within the church should heighten, not suppress, each person's individual particularity. God's goal is unity, not mere sameness. But they can remind us to teach our youth that we become individuals through concrete affiliations and commitments and not solely by following our inner desires and ambitions. Though the latter seem to arise from deep within the individual, they are often little more than a reflection of an unconscious mass fixation or the result of conscious marketing manipulation.

Progressive Christianity is concerned with important causes such as racial justice, care for the earth, and economic sharing. These endeavors all require a relational intuition of reality. Individual passion is not enough. As soon as it becomes "my cause," I too easily run into problems and too quickly run out of energy. Mother Teresa (now Saint Teresa of Calcutta) evidently understood these problems, as the following story illustrates.

A young man came to her and declared his desire to help: "Mother, I have a special vocation to work with the lepers. I want to give my life to them, my whole being. Nothing attracts me more than that."

She could see his sincerity. "I know for a fact that he truly loved those afflicted with leprosy," she recalled. Nevertheless, she gently chided him: "I, in turn, answered him, 'I think that you are somewhat wrong, Brother. Our vocation consists in belonging to Jesus. The work is nothing but a means to express our love for him. . . . What is important is for you to belong to Jesus. And he is the one who offers you the means to express that belonging.'"[2]

At first blush, it could appear Mother Teresa was denigrating this young man's passionate sense of vocation. But more accurately, she may

---

[2] Mother Teresa, *Mother Teresa: In My Own Words*, compiled by José Luis González-Balado (New York: Gramercy, 1997), 107.

have been trying to teach him to think relationally. We begin by recalling that charity work is hard to do, and the biggest hurdle is probably spiritual. The very word *charity* connotes the danger. We can picture the person with power and privilege reaching down to a weak and needy recipient. The one thinks, "It feels so good to help the unfortunate; I take such pride in doing what is right." The other, "I cannot afford to be proud." So we banish the word *charity* and in other ways update and monitor our language, without real rehabilitation. No wonder educators such as Paulo Freire sometimes reflected that the privileged have nothing worthwhile to offer the oppressed. A helping hand only replays the power dynamics of oppression.

Yet Mother Teresa has found a way to invert these dynamics. She starts by seeing herself in Jesus, belonging to him. The cross she wears signifies she is at one with Christ. She proceeds to see the poorest people of Calcutta as her "brothers and sisters" through Christ; and then, by the same logic, she comes to feel that in washing the feet of those afflicted with leprosy, she is washing the feet of Jesus. In this relational picture, they sit in the place of privilege, and she is humbled.

I have not interviewed all the people whose feet she washed, so I am not making empirical claims but rather describing spiritual logic. I am suggesting that this way of thinking—relationally—has practical import for the causes progressive Christian parents want their children to care about. Further, I am suggesting that relational thinking is not just a means toward the end of solving a pressing social or ecological problem; if we thought more relationally in the first place, we would not have the problem.

Meanwhile, evangelical parents face a slightly different set of challenges. Mother Teresa's language of "belonging to Jesus" comes naturally to them. My Sunday school teachers stressed the need to have a personal relationship with Christ, and I want my son likewise to learn what a friend he has in Jesus. But there are also two atonement facts I want him to see more clearly than I did. First, relationality includes the cross. Second, the cross has cosmic consequences.

Speaking of relationality, Paul says he has been crucified with Christ (Gal 2:20). He also says we have been buried with Christ in baptism (Rom

6:3). I'm not exactly sure why my teachers did not talk about being close and intimate with Christ in his death. It could be because death and intimacy are hard topics individually and harder still when brought together. But it could also be because Paul ties union with Christ in his death to baptism, and the "Romans road" of salvation usually took a detour around baptism. Let me try to explain.

Romans 6:23 says, "The wages of sin is death." In other words, if you work your whole life for sin, your final paycheck is death. In modern preaching, this metaphor gets reworked slightly to mean that if you are a sinner (and you are; see Rom 3:23), then death is your just penalty. A quick flip to the letter of Hebrews shows that Jesus took this penalty in our place, then a flip back to Romans 10:13 tells us how we can claim the free gift of salvation: "Everyone who calls upon the name of the Lord shall be saved."

And God bless everyone saved through this preaching! At the same time, I recall a premarital meeting where a young man told me why he did not feel a need to be involved with God or church. He had already gotten his salvation as a teenager. He had done that transaction. He told me (and I quote), "My ticket to heaven is already punched." Now, Pastor, could we get back to planning the wedding?

How should I have responded? Had I more courage and presence of mind, I might have said, "Yes, but were you crucified with Christ, and are you daily dying to sin? Were you buried with Jesus in his death, and are you now, *today* [emulating John Wesley here] putting to death those things that are killing your soul? Because if not, pretty soon they will start killing your future wife."

Romans 6 says plainly, "We have been buried with him by baptism into death" (6:4). But the "Romans road" to salvation avoided baptism, perhaps because evangelical preaching harking back to John Smyth and John Wesley has stressed the importance of heartfelt repentance and prayerful surrender over and against those who equated salvation with infant baptism.[3] Smyth and Wesley were not the first to warn that salvation cannot be turned into a transaction with water. As far back as the fourth

---

[3] Wesley held that infant baptism is salvific for infants.

century, Gregory of Nyssa told baptismal candidates that without the gift of the Holy Spirit and a transformed life, "the water is but water."[4]

Gregory was describing a real problem, but the solution is not to replace one transaction with another. The cross is not a business deal that lets us obtain the commodity of salvation. Even in Hebrews, sacrificial death meant transference more than transaction: atonement came through intimate connection.[5] Can we help young people see that a relationship with Jesus does not start after the cross, it starts on the cross or, in another sense, in the womb of Mary?

This topic is important because it connects to the problem of suffering. We do our best to keep our children from suffering. Still, suffering is built into the design of biological life as well as the nature of human consciousness. Yet every day, youth hear hundreds of social messages telling them that suffering is the main obstacle to their happiness. It would be good for them to hear once that suffering is sometimes the only path to joy.

Paul writes, "I want to know Christ and the power of his resurrection and the sharing of his sufferings by becoming like him in his death" (Phil 3:10). Suffering often makes individuals feel isolated. I become enclosed in my pain. But suffering can sometimes connect us with others who have likewise suffered. Evidently Paul's relational identity with Christ is so complete that he is willing (even wanting) to suffer for the same reasons Jesus did. From one perspective, Paul is a masochist, but from another, a realist who knows that suffering and resurrection power are intertwined. From still another perspective, he just wants to be close to Jesus.

Thinking about intimacy with Christ takes us back to the word's root meaning: innermost. Deep within the person (speaking spiritually, not biologically), in the innermost sanctum, the Holy of Holies, is where the Spirit of Christ is pleased to dwell. Intimacy can also take us in the direction of romance. In the Old Testament, Israel is God's spouse; in the New Testament, the church is Christ's bride; and in subsequent centuries, the motifs of marriage and romance have been both a tremendous blessing

---

[4] Gregory of Nyssa, "The Great Catechism," in *Nicene and Post-Nicene Fathers of the Christian Church*, vol. 5, trans. Philip Schaff and Henry Wace (New York: Christian Literature, 1893), 508.
[5] My thanks to Dr. Steven Schweitzer for this distinction between transaction and transference.

and curse to Christian devotion. The blessing results from romantic attraction being one of the most powerful motives a modern Western individual can experience, as adolescents and young adults especially can attest. Being in relationship with God involves this kind of passion, in more or less sublimated form. Evangelical and Pentecostal teaching and singing have long stressed the supreme worth of intimacy with God, from Charles Wesley's "Jesus, Lover of My Soul" to more recent offerings by Hillsong and Bethel.

But there is a downside. The romantic ideal can lead to a self-centered desire to have powerful feelings, a love of being in love, and it can lead the lovers to care less about the rest of creation. When, in literature, Anthony and Cleopatra are in each other's arms, their kingdoms go to pot—which may be okay as far as those fabled kingdoms go, but Jesus very much wants us to be concerned for the actual kingdom of God. In Romantic literature, "death" becomes a euphemism for sex, and by the same token, the physical death of the two lovers, often in each other's arms, makes complete their renunciation of the world, for the entire world is a small thing compared with the largeness of their love. They must leave the world because the world with its petty concerns and conventions does not understand true love. But now we are a far cry from Christ, who died for the life of the world, not as an escape from it.

We are also now in complicated territory. The relationship between devotion to Mary as *Regina Coeli* (Queen of Heaven) and the courtly love ideal of *la belle dame sans merci* (i.e., an incomparable, unattainable woman) was complex in the Middle Ages, as is the relationship between contemporary Christian music and the love songs of surrounding culture today. Hopefully the church is purifying, not just copying, the impulses of its cultural environment. But the challenge is stiff.

The solution to the problem lies in an expansion, not reduction, of intimacy. The scope of intimacy is greater than sex, eros, or romance. A scientist longs for intimate knowledge of subatomic particles. A parent is intimately aware of her infant's sleeping pattern, down to the rise and fall of each tiny yet momentous breath. Intimacy involves sensing and responding to an innermost reality.

When Paul speaks of being crucified with Christ or being buried with Christ in baptism, it is a portrayal of intimacy. At first, it is a picture of Jesus and me—an aspect of having a personal relationship with Jesus that I had overlooked. But gradually, if I come to see that I *am* that relationality, then I can begin to see things through Christ's eyes. I start to apprehend how the cross has cosmic consequences.

Jesus says, "Now is the judgment of this world; now the ruler of this world will be driven out. And I, when I am lifted up from the earth, will draw all people to myself" (John 12:31–32). Jesus is speaking here about the whole world (in Greek, *kosmos*). As John explains at the outset of the Gospel, Jesus is intimately involved with the world because "the world came into being through him" (John 1:10). However, "this world" is not that world—not the cosmos God created, as depicted in Genesis.

To be sure, "this world" is impressive. It has amassed unrivaled wealth and military might. "This world" has achieved technological marvels: viaducts, aqueducts, temples, coliseums. Yet "now is the judgment of this world"—"this world" now stands condemned because in crucifying Jesus, the world condemns itself.[6] The cross shows how far the world has fallen from the relational, purposeful, very good creation of Genesis. The cross demonstrates how much people have departed from God's design for human dominion. The cross reveals the final destination of the sin in the Garden, the ultimate outcome of the desire to be like God apart from God. It ends in killing God.

Every sin, says Schmemann, is a rejection of God, but the cross is the "decisive and all-embracing" rejection. It implicates the whole interconnected world, across time and place. It also implicates and brings to judgment Satan and other invisible forces that are intertwined with human evil. The cross judges the world and dethrones the ruler of this world.

The same cross also enthrones Christ as King.

In "And I, when I am lifted up," the double meaning of "lifted up" is striking. Both criminals and kings are lifted up. Through physical eyes,

---

[6] Alexander Schmemann, *Of Water and the Spirit: A Liturgical Study of Baptism* (Crestwood, NY: St. Vladimir's University Press, 1997), 89.

people see a crucifixion. Through eyes of the heart, Jesus and believers in him see a coronation. Isaiah, after King Uzziah died, also had a vision in which he saw the Lord lifted up and seated on a throne.

The soldiers mock Jesus with a crown of thorns. The followers of Jesus then search for centuries to find some relic from that thorn bush or some precious splinter from the true cross that became Christ's throne. And having found it, or something like it, they enshrine it in gold.

In choosing to be friends with God, we are also choosing the reality we see. Jesus tells his friends, "In a little while the world will no longer see me, but you will see me" (John 14:19). The Gospel of John depicts how seeing Jesus entails seeing a new creation that is taking place. The first letters of the Gospel, "In the beginning was the Word," are a clear echo of Genesis. Subsequent verses count off days and in other ways (Jesus making wine from water) allude to new creation. People have taken the creation depicted in Genesis and done their own thing. They and we have conspired with evil forces. They and we have used our big brains to construct our own order and purpose. They and we have developed our own ways of relating. The cross reveals how all our paths, apart from God, lead to death.

But the cross also epitomizes the new creation. In this creation, life is defined by the life that is in Jesus. This life enters the physical world, down to its subatomic particles. In this creation, love is defined by the love that is in Jesus, and this love is powerful. It causes him to lay down his life for his friends (John 15:13). This love even takes priority over physical properties, making it possible for Jesus to overcome physical death—indeed, making it impossible for death to keep its hold on him.

That is why Jesus died—so we can live together with God and so we can choose to be friends with God. As my son and daughter grow up and learn more about these things, I hope they can see how the "we" is an intimate relationality with cosmic consequences.

Paradigm Shifts

I n an age of science, it is normal to think that new means improved. New insights of science are more advanced, new instruments of technology more useful (usually). Who would rather still be using their first phone or computer?

But the ancient world took a dimmer view of novelty. New meant suspect. New things had not stood the test of time. To thrive today, youth need both new knowledge and old wisdom. In calling the relational reading of Genesis "new and ancient" in chapter 23, I had hoped to signal that novelty is not the chief aim in teaching young people. The goal is rather to arrive at a place where we can say, "It seemed good to the Holy Spirit and to us."

The "us" refers not only to a group gathered in some physical space but also to the church as a whole—a mystical community of people both here and abroad, both living and dead. The aim of the ecumenical councils, starting in Acts 15, was to catch the collective sense of where God was leading them.

It seems fair to ask, therefore, how this book's attempt to relate faith and science would fare with an audience of ancient Hebrews or early Christians. Though we cannot interview them directly, we can imagine, as a thought experiment, how they might respond. This kind of exercise can help to demonstrate how faith and science should be in dialogue. In some previous chapters, the intent was to keep biological formation distinct from spiritual creation and in general to separate faith and science. But the pattern of Chalcedon calls for a relational unity, or a unified relationality. We don't want to confuse faith and science, but we do want to connect them into a coherent vision of reality.

In the dialogue between science and theology, science can offer insights that amplify our sense of reality and sometimes modify our reading of Scripture. To show this dialogue in action, let's start with the fairly easy example discussed earlier. The Bible says in several places that the earth is fixed and immovable (1 Sam 2:8; 1 Chr 16:30; Ps 93:1; Ps 96:10; Ps 104:5; Isa 45:18). For centuries, the people who wrote and heard these words did not realize the earth was moving—rotating on its axis at a speed of about one thousand miles per hour (at the equator) and also orbiting the sun at a speed of sixty-seven thousand miles per hour. They probably imagined the earth was moving at zero miles per hour because it was fixed on pillars.

As a thought experiment, what would happen if we transported ancient Hebrews or early Christians to a science classroom of today and explained to them the motion of the earth? Our ancient visitors might reply along these lines:

> This information is good. It modifies but does not undermine what we have believed. We were not reading the Bible to learn how to grow barley or make pruning hooks. We were reading it to learn how God relates to us and all creation. The fixity of the earth told us of God's sovereignty and reliability, and it spoke of how God's decrees are firm and permanent.
>
> Now you tell us amazing things—of stars hurtling through space, going a billion cubits an hour, and of the earth speeding around the sun. You tell us this great velocity is actually required to keep us grounded: if the earth were to stop moving, then all our sheep and cattle and people would fly up instantly into the atmosphere. And so we praise God for the motion that lets us *experience* the earth as fixed

and immovable, the motion that lets us watch the sun descend over the horizon from a place of quietude and peace. This motion points us back to God.

This reading is relational because it relates faith and science and also because it looks continually for what the Bible says about God's ongoing relationship with us. This reading keeps in mind that when biblical writers are describing the physical world, they are saying how it looks to the naked eye, how the world comes to us in human experience. Still today, we say that the sun rises and the sun sets, though scientifically we know better.

The dialogue with science does not mean we need to give up every article of faith that science cannot validate. Even scientists who are atheists may choose to hold beliefs for which there is no scientific basis (e.g., that life has meaning, that love has value). For most Christians, the bodily resurrection of Jesus has been central to the gospel message. Science cannot explain this event. Is it scientifically impossible? Scientists seldom use the word *impossible*, for they realize how much of reality exceeds their grasp. But clearly the eyes of modern science are apt to view reports of resurrection with skepticism.

People in the days of Jesus did not need modern science to figure out that dead people tend to stay dead. Many people initially rejected the message of resurrection on grounds of common sense. Yet many others accepted it due to eyewitness testimonies and personal encounters with the risen Christ. As a thought experiment, what would happen if we transported some of those early believers into a science classroom of today and explained the neurological and cardiological reasons why reviving someone after three days is not scientifically feasible?

We don't have to guess the answer. The apostle Paul has already told us. If the dead cannot be raised, then even Christ was not raised. And if Christ was not raised, then our faith is in vain (1 Cor 15:12–17). The ancient visitors might add, "We believed then and still believe now that God's presence transcends the physical realm and God's power transforms the human body. The working of this mighty power is what raised Jesus from the dead, and one day it will raise us too."

We can maintain this same stance today and still highly value what science tells us about the human body. Medical science offers immense help in caring for our bodies in the normal course of events. At the same time, Christian faith claims that God's higher-order activity can enter the physical frame to reorder the normal course of events. In the dialogue between faith and science, faith appeals to this nonscientific frame of reference to embrace some facts that science cannot fathom.

This dynamic back-and-forth interchange between science and faith requires what is commonly called a paradigm shift. But it does not discredit science. We can find an analogy for this shift within science itself, in the mental jump from the physics of Newton to that of Einstein. A paradigm shift is required to see space and time as being relative to the speed of light. It is sometimes said Einstein overruled Newton, but this statement is misleading. People who design cars, bridges, and all manner of technological instruments rely on Newton's theories all the time. These theories tell them very well what to expect in the normal course of events, with objects of the size and speed we typically encounter. In moving to the physics of Einstein, scientists do not abandon Newton.

So, too, by analogy, in moving from the science of physics to the metaphysics of Christian faith—in moving from an impersonal physical universe to a Christ-centered cosmos—we do not lose sight of science. In hoping for bodily resurrection, we still rely on medical science to care for the body. Christians built some of the world's first hospitals. That God valued the human body enough to inhabit one was a good reason to care for the bodies of fellow humans. Similarly, that God valued the physical universe enough to create it was a good reason to explore its myriad facts and facets.

The analogy of Newton and Einstein will offend some scientists, who question whether faith has any right in the first place to be "in dialogue" with science. After all, in moving from Newton to Einstein, we are still dealing with evidence that is physical. Where is the evidence for this second move, from scientific physics to Christian metaphysics?

There are two ways to reply. For some people, the idea that Christianity lacks evidence is based on an overall material view of reality. In this view, only physical evidence counts because only physical things really exist. In reply, we can graciously remind people who hold this view that there is still no scientific evidence to support it. Science can explore all sorts of physical things, but science cannot prove the nonexistence of nonphysical things. Materialism is a decision, not a discovery. It comes from a prior metaphysical commitment.

Other people will readily acknowledge that we all hold some kind of metaphysical commitment and are simply wondering how Christians support theirs. Why move from physics to the metaphysics of Christian faith? In reply, we can say most of the evidence for this paradigm shift is not scientific, but that does not automatically make it irrational or unpersuasive. While stories such as the following do not constitute scientific proofs, they do disclose how faith has its own kind of logic.

Rachel, an emerging adult in her late teens, was raised in a secular home but became intrigued by Christian beliefs. She recounted some of these beliefs to me in conversation one evening—that a man named Jesus performed miracles, that he died on a cross, was raised after three days, and more. She wanted to know whether I, as an actual specimen of a Christian, believed these things. I said that I did.

"No offense," she said, "but those ideas sound irrational, and you seem like an intelligent person."

"None taken," I reassured her.

She was still curious. *Why* did I believe these things? Was it simply that I had been taught them as a child? She herself had not been so taught.

I asked Rachel whether she ever prayed. She said that she did—every day, in fact, since she belonged to a twelve-step program and praying was part of the recovery plan. (Interestingly, one-fifth of atheists report that they sometimes pray.[1]) I suggested an experiment. During prayer, she could talk to God about Jesus: Was he the Son of God, did he die on a cross, was he resurrected? She could ask whatever questions came to mind. I suggested praying along these lines for three days.

[1] Joseph O. Baker and Buster G. Smith, *American Secularism: Cultural Contours of Nonreligious Belief Systems* (New York: New York University Press, 2015), 89.

About six months later, I got a phone message from a friend, inviting me to Rachel's baptism. I went. Afterward, she came up to me, still patting her wet hair with a towel, to report what had transpired during her prayer experiment.

After three days, she observed nothing. She decided, however, that three days was not a long enough time frame. In the twelve-step world of addiction recovery, thirty days was considered a good trial period. She continued to present her questions in prayer to whomever might be listening. Near the end of thirty days, her evidence arrived. As she was walking across the university campus, a stranger passed by, walking the other way. The stranger was wearing a T-shirt with a slogan imprinted on it. I don't remember the words or even if she told me, but the ideology of these words stood for what she hated. The words emblazoned on the shirt expressed a sentiment that was flatly wrong, and ordinarily it would have inflamed in her an intense anger toward this stranger.

But instead, on this particular day, she found herself overcome by an amazing kind of love. The love seemed to pour in from beyond her, and it poured out toward this other person she had never seen before. The love was stronger than anything she could explain, an alien force. For the rest of the day, she was—as the saying goes and as she herself said—walking on air, elevated by the power of this love. And this event was how she knew her prayer had been answered. This was her proof of Jesus's resurrection. She sensed he was the source of this love.

But what kind of proof is this? It is certainly not scientific. In terms of science, her experiment in prayer proves nothing. But in terms of how a person chooses to live her life, it changes everything. It would be easy, in an age of science, for a person to doubt this kind of evidence, even for Rachel herself to doubt it in later years. Yet we do make many choices in life—who to marry, where to live, what work to do—without a firm scientific basis. It is not scientific, but it is also not irrational to experience love that is life changing or to love even our enemies or to believe that Jesus Christ is risen from the dead. We could call it all wishful thinking. But just because things are dearly wished for does not make them automatically untrue.

Rachel had a personal experience, and personal experience is prob-ably always a component of faith. However, when people talk about their strongest reasons for believing in the resurrection or in other tenets of faith, they may name as evidence their prior belief in the Bible or in the church. Evidence and faithful reasoning are largely internal to the Bible and the church.

Accordingly, it will be good to ask what the church, down through the ages, might say about our proposed reading of Genesis—a reading that distinguishes and then unites material creation and relational creation. In the dialogue between faith and science, we can invite some ancient believ-ers to join us.

CHAPTER 29

Antioch and Alexandria

J esus refers to Jonah. He says, "As Jonah was three days and three nights in the belly of the sea monster, so for three days and three nights the Son of Man will be in the heart of the earth" (Matt 12:40).

Peter refers to Noah. He says Noah built an ark that saved eight people through the water, and this event is similar to baptism, since "baptism now saves you . . . as an appeal to God for a clean conscience" (1 Pet 3:21).

The physical drama of Jonah's fish or Noah's ark is what catches the attention of children and sparks their imagination. God uses the visible realm to build our faith in the invisible, said John Calvin.[1] At the same time, Jesus and Peter do not elaborate on physical details of what happened to Jonah and Noah; they say nothing about the fish's length or ark's depth. The focus falls rather on what these events tell us about the Son of Man and about baptism. What matters most is the meaning of these events for their audiences' current relationship with God. "What matters most here?" is a good question to ask whenever we read Scripture.

As students of church history may recall, the cities of Alexandria and Antioch represented two ways of reading the Bible during the first centuries. In Alexandria, a place of wealth and education, philosophers walked

---

[1] John Calvin, *Institutes of the Christian Religion*, ed. John T. McNeil, trans. Ford Lewis Battles (Philadelphia: Westminster, 1960), 1278.

the streets, and the Alexandrian school of interpretation reached its pinnacle or excess in the person of Origen.

Origen's mind leaped immediately to deeper meaning, which is what mattered most to him. He did not believe that creation as depicted in Genesis actually happened in history. He did not, among other things, find it credible that there could be three days without sun, moon, or stars. He believed other portions of the Bible were historically accurate, and overall these historically accurate portions outnumbered those that were not. But historical truth was not his primary concern. He was looking for timeless truth.

Origen's imagination led him to read allegorically, and this ability enabled him to make some hard passages more palatable. For example, Psalm 137 ("By the rivers of Babylon we sat down and wept") ends with a shocking prayer for vengeance against Israel's captors: "Happy is the one who repays you [Babylon] for what you have done to us. Happy is the one who seizes your little ones and dashes them against the rocks" (v. 8 NIV). In Septuagint manuscripts, the last word is singular: against the "rock" (not "rocks," plural). This word, Origen reasoned, stands for Christ, since 1 Corinthians 10:3 states clearly that Christ is the Rock. Babylon stands for the kingdom of evil, and the "little ones" refers to our little sins. Sin always starts out little, before it grows large and unmanageable. So happiness resides in bringing those little sins to Christ, for when dashed against the Rock, sin gets obliterated. Sneer if you will—it still sounds better than smashing babies.

In general, the readers of Alexandria held that one should reject the literal sense of any passage that would report God as doing something unworthy of God as well as any that contained inconsistencies or historical improbabilities.

North of the Egyptian city of Alexandria stood the ancient Greek city of Antioch. The Bible interpreters of Antioch took a different tack. They began with the literal or factual meaning. They were focused on how God moves in human history. At the same time, the readers of Antioch, no less than those of Alexandria, wanted to find truth beneath the surface. Jerome (347–420) summed up the Antiochene approach when he said that everything written in the Bible took place and at the same time has a deeper meaning. The literal meaning is not the deepest, but it is the first, the starting point. The deeper meaning is built on the literal, not opposed to it. This literal historical approach was taken up by subsequent Christian thinkers. It is found in Thomas Aquinas and in leading theologians of the Reformation. It became the church's chief exegetical method.[2]

Now it needs to be noted that this little narrative contrasting Antioch and Alexandria might itself be historically inaccurate. Though taught to generations of seminary students, it has been challenged by more recent patristic scholarship. However, to take an "Alexandrian" outlook, the ancient cities of Antioch and Alexandria represent two impulses that lie within each Christian: the desire to see God acting in the physical world and the desire to glimpse truth that transcends the physical-temporal sphere. The impulse of Alexandria pushes us speedily toward allegorical interpretations, particularly when the Bible speaks of God doing something deemed unworthy of God. But the sensibility of Antioch says we should stop to take things at face value before presuming to search for deeper meaning.

Both impulses are seen in the influential writings of Augustine, who favored an allegorical approach in his early theology but in later life came to see more and more passages of Scripture as being historical. All the early church thinkers would have agreed that the Bible has layers of meaning. By the sixteenth century, these four layers could be expressed in stanza form:

> The letter shows us what God and our forebears did;
> the allegory shows us where our faith is hid;
> the moral meaning gives us rules of daily life;
> the anagogy shows us where we end our strife.[3]

A classic example of the fourfold approach is a reading of Galatians 4 that sees Jerusalem having these four meanings:

---

[2] David Tracy and Robert McQueen Grant, *A Short History of the Interpretation of the Bible* (Minneapolis: Fortress Press, 2005).
[3] Tracy and Grant, *A Short History*, 85.

Historically, Jerusalem is the city of the Jews;

allegorically, it is the church of Christ;

morally, it signifies the human soul;

and anagogically, it points to the heavenly city that is the mother of us all.[4]

We can grasp these layers. We also find, as children of our times, that science influences our own sense of what matters most. We gravitate toward the earthly Jerusalem—the location that we can see with our physical eyes and excavate with our physical instruments. What can we learn about the people who lived there long ago? What blocks of stone or shards of pottery give evidence? We believe, scientifically, that this kind of investigation will lead us closer to the truth about Jerusalem.

In another century, believers were more focused on the heavenly Jerusalem. They read the Bible for anagogy—spiritual interpretations that would inform them about the afterlife. They wanted to dig deeper than the physical eye could see in order to glimpse eternity and so anticipate their own destiny. Some of their concerns are worth reclaiming with young people today. We can value the scientific sensibility, with all its wonderful benefits and at the same time appreciate how conversation with people of the past, as well as global believers today, can help youth reclaim a level of vision—eyes of the heart—that a Western scientific focus tends to screen out.

As a thought experiment, therefore, what would happen if we asked early church believers to weigh the ideas we have been talking about? How might they view neo-Darwinian evolution and Walton's proposal to read Genesis in terms of relational creation rather than physical creation?

It's safe to say that Darwin's theories would pose no problem to Origen and others of the so-called Alexandrian school. These believers were already disinclined to view Genesis 1–3 as a record of physical history, and it's easy to imagine them plunging readily into a discussion of relational creation. The relational reading elucidates why the world

---

[4] Tracy and Grant, *A Short History*, 85.

exists and the place of humanity within the divine order. It sets the stage for themes of spiritual life and death that recur throughout the Bible— deeper meanings the Alexandrians love to probe.

The Christians of Antioch should be equally receptive to these deeper meanings. But unlike the Alexandrians, they might be troubled, at least initially, by the ideas of Darwin, given their historical reading of Genesis 1–3. They would want physical truth to provide the foundation for spiritual truth. Yet the ancient Hebrew understanding of *bara'* might be just the kind of insight they would welcome. It would let them see their way past the conflict with modern science. If "create" does not entail manipulating molecules but rather endowing the physical world with order, meaning, and purpose, then the Christians of Antioch could teach their youth that Genesis is a literal, actual history of the week when God moved into the cosmos to make it a home, the week when the earth became God's holy temple.

As we have seen, this view of creation involves more than retranslating one word in the Bible. It requires rethinking our spiritual origins. It might be hard for the believers of Antioch to agree that God intended death, and therefore suffering, to be part of the original cosmic order. Suffering and death could be obstacles for them, as they were for young Charles Darwin, as they are for Christians today.

But honestly, suffering and death are obstacles no matter what. We simply become accustomed to certain narratives and so stop asking questions. Many Christians currently hold a mental framework whereby Adam and Eve are placed in a perfect garden but nearly right away commence to disobey. The days of death-free bliss are pitifully short, the years of subsequent suffering interminably long. Why such a painful imbalance? If all this suffering is a consequence of human freedom, why not create humans who are more freely like Christ from the start? And if Christ was, from the start, the intended solution, why not send him to earth sooner? And if his final return spells the end of suffering, why not send him back sooner still, before the Holocaust or before another child succumbs to cancer?

Our minds recoil not at the mere existence of suffering but at the horrific extent of suffering and the extent of evil that humans intentionally inflict on one another. Much suffering is incomprehensible; some is unbearable. There will always be questions, but it's worth pointing out that our questions are usually based on Christian premises, in that we take for granted God's all-powerful goodness and benevolence toward us. We take for granted that human life has great value and that human minds are allowed to question God.

The reading of Genesis on the table does offer a different twist. It says human disobedience is not solely responsible for suffering. Human sin does not solely cause all the earthquakes, devastation, and death in the world. Yes, when humans fall from grace, the environment suffers, as we see in Genesis 3. When people depart from God's will, it intensifies suffering and death. But in the new or ancient view being proposed, we don't start with a perfect world in which humans are the sole problem. We start with a good but incomplete world in which God appoints humans to play a central role in the solution—as God's agents of care and transformation, as defeaters of evil and conveyers of God's goodness in the world, as Christ's fellow victors over death and death's dominion. Via humanity, God is bringing the cosmos to completion.

This royal, priestly, prophetic vocation summons all our considerable creativity. It summons both the energy of prayer and the energy of scientific ingenuity. We are called to relieve suffering and to overthrow the powers of sin, death, and the devil. This work also summons the idealism and passion of each new generation, who desire to see the world made new. This is God's goal, and they are God's agents.

Before finishing the discussion of Darwin with young people, we must address a loose end—more accurately, a gaping question. The foregoing chapters have offered a way to teach young people that there is no necessary conflict between the Bible and the biological theory of origins held by professional scientists. However, this peace does not extend to every way that neo-Darwinian theory is taught to young people today. Around the time of the *Scopes* trial, many young people were being taught that eugenics was good Darwinian social policy. That danger has receded today, but neo-Darwinian theory may be put to ill use in other ways. So if a young person asks whether evolution is compatible with Christianity, the answer is not always a simple yes or no.

CHAPTER 30

Evolution Means What Now?

To what does "evolution" refer? What does evolution explain? Many people, including most scientists, would say neo-Darwinian theories of evolution give an account of physical processes that still leave ample room for spiritual dimensions of reality. If evolution is simply good science, then it is compatible with Christianity, especially given the reading of Genesis and Romans just proffered.

Though young-earth creationists take a material view of creation in Genesis, they, too, currently accept (nay, embrace) natural selection and other evolutionary mechanisms while clearly rejecting a full-scale particles-to-people biological theory. But even if we move all the way from particles to people, we have not necessarily moved beyond the physical realm. However, there is an unlimited version of neo-Darwinian theory that claims evolution explains all of life, visible and invisible, physical and spiritual. And the more this version portrays evolution as the deepest, best, and truest account of what is really "going on" in life, the more it runs counter to the faith of most Christians, across the progressive-to-conservative spectrum.

In this view, evolution becomes a theory of everything, and science gives way to scientism. If it is held that everything, including belief in God, can be explained in terms of survival benefits, then the path of faith grows incredibly narrow, and it leads to destruction. Scientists who are believing Christians would hardly take this tack. Yet in an age of science, materialistic and utilitarian notions hang in the air like secondhand smoke and seep into our daily conversation.

For example, a youth leader may say, "It's good to have faith because your faith really helps you cope with tough times in life." Perhaps the youth leader intends only to convey that psychological resilience is one of God's many blessings. But the young person may hear a different message, which says that faith is a mental crutch for those who need it. Why? In part because evolutionary theory can give rise to a worldview in which religion and everything else are tied to adaptation and survival. In this view, Jesus came that we might have an abundant coping mechanism.

Evolution as a theory of everything would be opposed by Christians in both Antioch and Alexandria as well as most locations around the world today. Of course, it does not need to become a theory of everything, but the scientific theory arose in the nineteenth century, an era of grand universals and intellectual attempts to explain all things without reference to God. Marx tried to explain all human behavior, including religion, in terms of economic motives, and Freud at one point tried to explain everything in terms of the sex drive. Darwin was a naturalist, but it did not take long for some followers to mishandle his biological theory by turning it into racist social ideas. Nor was Darwin himself immune to this pitfall, straying as he did from beetles and finches to speculations about the "favored races" of humanity and how in time the gap between the favored and unfavored races of humans would grow as wide as the present gap between people and apes.

Those are sins of the past, which may have been passed on. But also pertinent for today is the fact that many people who strongly disavow evolution as a basis for racism will still employ it as the basis for their materialism. Here we are talking about the kind of materialism that is not just a method for science but also a vision of all reality. Evolutionary biology becomes for some people the foundation for supposing that all human life can be reduced to physical drives, ultimately the drive to survive, and then, if we turn from biology to physics, everything is reducible to physical matter and motion. Angels, demons, and every other spiritual thing are cast as fictions conjured by molecules of the brain, which enlightened people do well to dispel through science. Whatever adaptation and survival function these religious fictions may have served in the past, we can live longer and better without them today—so goes this line of reasoning. Yet faith recoils against this reducing tendency, this overexcited use of Occam's razor, in which evolution is presumed to explain everything.

In short, the problem occurs when the discoveries of physical evolution morph into a decision for metaphysical materialism. This point is one arrow in the creationist quiver that hits its intended target. And if there is one evolutionary biologist whom creationists love to quote, it is Richard Lewontin, because he has made this exact point for them and done so with rhetorical flair. His oft-cited book review, titled "Billions and Billions of Demons," recalls the evening he teamed up with Carl Sagan to debate young-earth creationists.

In an auditorium in Little Rock, Arkansas, Lewontin and Sagan, two Jewish atheists, took the debating stage to press the case for evolution in front of an "immense audience of creationist fundamentalist Christians." Lewontin reports the outcome:

> We were, in fact, well treated, but despite our absolutely compelling arguments, the audience unaccountably voted for the opposition. . . . Sagan and I drew different conclusions from our experience. For me the confrontation between creationism and the science of evolution was an example of historical, regional, and class differences in culture that could only be understood in the context of American social history. For Carl it was a struggle between ignorance and knowledge, although it is not clear to me what he made of the unimpeachable scientific credentials of our opponent, except perhaps to see him as an example of the Devil quoting scripture.[1]

---

[1] Richard C. Lewontin, "Billions and Billions of Demons," *New York Review of Books*, January 9, 1997.

Their creationist opponent had a PhD in zoology from a prestigious university. The "scripture" to which Lewontin refers is the evidence supporting evolution, which their opponent had sought to undermine. But as Lewontin explains, the debate is not simply a question of religious ignorance versus scientific knowledge. For many of the proponents on the "science" side have their own metaphysical agenda. Lewontin sees Sagan's book *The Demon-Haunted World: Science as a Candle in the Dark* as an example of physical science morphing into metaphysical dogma. Sagan's goal is to promote an entire worldview. In Lewontin's words, he wants people "to reject irrational and supernatural explanations of the world, the demons that exist only in their imaginations, and to accept a social and intellectual apparatus, Science, as the only begetter of truth."

Lewontin himself happens to share Sagan's metaphysical conviction. He too has a fully material view of reality. But unlike Sagan, he recognizes that this view is a decision—a prior assumption and religious-like commitment. It is Sagan's and his chosen starting place, not an inevitable destination at which one arrives by following scientific evidence. He writes, "It is not that the methods and institutions of science somehow compel us to accept a material explanation of the phenomenal world, but, on the contrary, that we are forced by our *a priori* adherence to material causes to create an apparatus of investigation and a set of concepts that produce material explanations, no matter how counter-intuitive, no matter how mystifying to the uninitiated. Moreover, that materialism is absolute, for we cannot allow a Divine Foot in the door." Lewontin returns to the theme of science and culture and—in 1997—makes this prescient remark: "The struggle for possession of public consciousness between material and mystical explanations of the world is one aspect of the history of the confrontation between elite culture and popular culture."

To work within Lewontin's terms, elite culture inclines toward a material explanation of the world, and popular culture toward a mystical explanation. On the surface, confessing Christians would probably all agree they hew toward a "mystical explanation." But Christians who are members of elite culture also share many "material explanation" sensibilities.

Episcopalian pastors, for example, may think twice before preaching on spiritual warfare or divine healing.

The American "history of confrontation" between elite and popular cultures has parallels in other times and places, since gaps between rich and poor are nothing new. Alexandria was a much wealthier city than Antioch, which may be one reason the people of Alexandria are said to have preferred philosophical interpretations of Scripture. They did not feel an urgent need to see God's hand moving in human history. When people feel they can prosper well enough on their own, it tends to enervate prayers for God to intervene in the material realm. Divine intervention may come across more as meddling.

Today, these sorts of cultural differences complicate the creation-and-evolution debate. Picture two young people, both Christians, meeting on a college campus. One comes from an elite culture background and accepts evolution on the authority of scientists without bothering to study any of the details. The other has been homeschooled in a curriculum replete with creation science and in this sense is much better versed in evolutionary theory. However, the elite culture Christian insinuates the creationist is uneducated and backward, while the creationist implies the evolutionist is not really a believing Christian. Or more amicably, they just decide everyone is different and any view on anything is a matter of personal opinion.

We have been looking for a way forward that does not involve this kind of insinuation, disparagement, or avoidance of discourse altogether. Toward this end, a model for relating theology and science has been proposed. This model, in keeping with the pattern of Chalcedon, says the two disciplines are distinct in their knowledge but unified in their truth. When in dialogue, theology and science can complement and even correct each other.

The test case for implementing this model has been creation and evolution. The science of evolution prompted us to reread Genesis and Romans through eyes of the heart and with a view to how ancient audiences would have heard God's Word. This proposal for rereading creation needs to stand or fall on biblical evidence. And if it stands, we find the ancient reading has remarkable contemporary relevance.

Meanwhile, scientific theories of evolution must stand or fall on scientific evidence. But even if they stand firmly, we can still teach youth not to reduce reality to the physical realm. Both the first living cells and human consciousness are hard to explain in physical terms. Further, even if and when these things *are* explained in purely physical terms, we can remind young people that an explanation can be accurate without being adequate. For there is more to life and death than meets the eye—the physical eye, that is. They, like we, long to see through eyes of the heart.

We keep in mind this basic point: that God is not a placeholder we use to fill gaps in physical explanations. Rather, Christian faith offers young people, and us, a way to read all of reality. If physical black dots on white paper are made blacker and clearer than ever, it does not prevent the dots from transforming invisibly into words. In fact, for those who learn how to read, it makes the reading that much easier. Similarly, the mind enlightened by physical science can read God's handiwork in nature all the more clearly.

This analogy is helpful, if not perfect. For there is this hindrance to seeing the universe as God's handiwork: as young people study science and utilize technology, it invariably bends their minds in the physical direction. They will need reminding, as we all do, that metaphysical materialism is still a decision they can forgo.

Nowhere does science prove the nonexistence of nonmaterial things. A decision for materialism (of both the metaphysical and consumerist varieties) will feel less like common sense if our minds are also guided into thinking spiritually—through Bible reading, prayer, testimony, worshipful singing, intimate conversation, experiences of sublime beauty, works of justice, acts of compassion, and every other item that makes up the Christian life. All of these activities, done in ways that "seem good to the Holy Spirit and to us," will open our eyes more widely to see the deep things of God more clearly. For those who have ears to hear, baptism and Holy Communion especially speak volumes about how God's relational creation transforms the material world.

A Monk and His Peas

Somewhere in size between the Big Infinity and Little Infinity lies the pea. Most people know peas as a food item, fresh or frozen, but for Gregor Mendel, the pea was an object of care and devotion. "Would you like to see my children?" the celibate priest asked his visitors, before escorting them to his glass house, where he grew an estimated twenty-eight thousand pea plants.[1]

From these plants, Gregor counted and sorted as many as three hundred thousand individual peas.[2] Some peas were smooth, some wrinkled. Some pods were yellow, some green. Some plants flowered at the top, some all along the stem. Focusing on these and four other pairs of traits, he recorded each pea generation as meticulously as a medieval monk copying biblical genealogies in a scriptorium.

As students of biology may recall, Mendel acted like a monk because he was a monk—specifically, a friar in an Augustinian order, living in Moravia in the nineteenth century. A divine order suffused his life, and likewise, in his cross-pollinations of pea plants, Mendel trusted that the

---

[1] Robin Marantz Henig, *The Monk in the Garden: The Lost and Found Genius of Gregor Mendel, the Father of Genetics* (Boston: Houghton Mifflin, 2000), 119. Cf. Simon Mawer, *Gregor Mendel: Planting the Seeds of Genetics* (New York: Abrams in association with the Field Museum of Chicago, 2006), 43.

[2] Mawer, *Gregor Mendel*, 9.

variations were not random but instead had a hidden physical order waiting to be discovered.

Some traits were dominant, others recessive, but in either case, Mendel proposed that visible traits were caused by an invisible *Merkmal* (character) or *Anlage* (factor) residing within the plant cells.[3] He fished for the right word because the words *gene* and *genetics* did not yet exist. Before genetics emerged as a branch of science, people used the term *Mendelism* to refer to the unseen force at work in cells.[4] Even this word *Mendelism* did not arise until thirty years after Gregor Mendel's death, when scientists reread his papers and were able to grasp their significance. During his lifetime, he worked in relative obscurity.

Today, genes and DNA (the carrier of genetic information) are the locale of medical breakthroughs, the frontier of research in a hundred other fields, and a metaphor for the fundamental stuff of life in an information age. But in Mendel's day, people did not appreciate, nor could he himself foresee, that his study of inheritance was unlocking the door that would lead down the corridors of time to the discovery of DNA. Some science historians suppose he was just a clever monk who had a knack for botany.[5]

This belittling depiction hardly seems fair if we compare Mendel with another towering scientist of the nineteenth century, Charles Darwin. Mendel was able to do something Darwin could not, which was to translate his theory into the most scientific of all languages—mathematics. There were other differences between the two men. Darwin came from a family of wealth and never lacked for funding or publicity. Mendel grew up in a family that faced bitter poverty even before he took his monastic vow of lifelong poverty.

Accordingly, the two men inhabited different spheres of social power. When Alfred Russel Wallace hit upon the basic mechanisms of evolution at the same time Darwin was working out the details of his theory, Darwin's influential friends at the Linnean Society convinced young Wallace to delay publication of his findings so Darwin could finish a paper that

[3] Mawer, *Gregor Mendel*, 81.
[4] Mawer, *Gregor Mendel*, 102.
[5] Henig, *The Monk in the Garden*, 5.

would ensure both men received joint credit for the discovery. By comparison, when Mendel wrote to a professor at the University of Munich, humbly asking the esteemed professor to review his research on heredity, he received curt replies that implied his ideas were not too significant. Yet some of these ideas were evidently good enough for the esteemed professor to publish in his own book, without giving credit to Mendel.

Along with their differences, Darwin and Mendel shared certain traits. Both gravitated toward the study of theology, which in their century was far from an odd coincidence, since naturalism, as an empirical discipline, was still connected to the theoretical discipline of natural theology. Even if the fields of science and theology were quickly drifting apart, the universe of knowledge held them together for the time being.

Though these and other Christian roots of Western science are much less visible today, the fact remains that Mendel was a Christian first and scientist second. His biographers unfailingly mention he was a monk but skirt any potential connection between his faith and his science. They concede that the church did not impede his work, but that seems to be the best thing anyone can say about Gregor's religion. Perhaps his Christian faith made him more kind, some writers allow. "We all loved Mendel," one of his students recalled after his death.[6] During his life, the Augustinian monk whom they all loved kept little record of his theological thinking. Any connection, say, between Mendel's ideas and those of Augustine would be pure speculation.

Yet biographers do not shrink from speculating in other areas. Depression, they surmise, is what led Mendel to spend a year at home, mostly in bed, at age seventeen. Anxiety over exams, they speculate, is the reason he failed twice to advance beyond the rank of substitute teacher.[7] But what shaped his mind to think about inheritance?

Centuries prior to Mendel, the investigation of inheritance focused mainly on the problem of human sin. It was observed that people tend to be selfish—curved in on themselves, as Augustine had put it. Whether

---

[6] Henig, *The Monk in the Garden*, 92.
[7] Mawer, *Gregor Mendel*, 41; Henig, *The Monk in the Garden*, 61.

this curvature of the soul is caused by "concupiscence" (harmful desire) or something else, the debate in Augustine's day centered on heredity. Augustine's opponent Pelagius claimed that the trait of sinful behavior was learned by imitation; it came from a sinful environment—from nurture more than nature. But Augustine said the trait came from "propagation not imitation."[8] It was passed down invisibly from one generation to the next.

Obviously, Augustine did not set forth a full-blown theory of genetics, but then neither did Mendel. What the two men shared was a frame of mind. Though dealing with very different issues of heredity, they both approached their problem by proposing that an invisible factor could cause visible traits, and it could reside at the base of an organism even before birth. It was related somehow to the very act of procreation. Both male and female parents contributed to this factor. Using the sexuality of plants, Mendel demonstrated that male and female parents contribute equally to their offspring. In regard to humans, this fact was still doubted by some biologists in his day, who gave inflated importance to the male seed.[9]

In short, Mendel's study of theology may have made him a better scientist. His understanding of Augustine may have helped him make genetic discoveries in biology, just as knowledge of Christ's two natures may have inspired Niels Bohr to formulate the principle of complementarity in physics.

In prior chapters, I challenged the idea that sin is a biological inheritance in order to place more focus on sin as a spiritual force at work in the world. The initial sin of Adam and Eve ruptures their relationship with God, and the effect ripples into all their other relationships. But this sin did not bring physical death into the physical universe, nor is it the reason people die today. This is the main point I was trying to make: death is part of this physical universe and part of human existence—save for the tree of life, save for the medicine of immortality, save for the salvation of Christ.

---

[8] Philip Schaff, *Saint Augustine's Anti-Pelagian Works* (Edinburgh: T & T Clark, 1886).
[9] Mawer, *Gregor Mendel*, 13.

But this point need not be overstated. Adam's sin brought spiritual death, which in turn led back to physical death. The spiritual and physical are thus intimately intertwined. Pertinent to discussions of heredity, the Bible suggests that parents and grandparents pass on spiritual as well as physical traits to their offspring. Paul tells Timothy that he has inherited the faith of his mother and grandmother, Lois and Eunice. Faith is likewise found in the offspring of Abraham and Sarah, alongside character defects such as the tendency to use deception and trickery in response to fear. Timothy and Jacob may have acquired faith through biological heredity (nature), their home environment (nurture), or most likely some combination of both. In any case, it is very clear parents and grandparents have enormous influence in the spiritual lives of their offspring, for good or ill, and whether they realize it or not. The largest study ever conducted on American youth and their spiritual lives draws the simple conclusion that "parents matter most."[10]

Yet pastors and youth pastors also have a vital part to play in their interactions with youth and families. Mendel grew up in a church environment that was conducive to scientific pursuits. What are we, for our part, telling young people today? Is science the friend of faith or its foe? We are telling them something, one way or the other, in the messages we deliver from the pulpit or through informal conversation. Mendel's biological theory tells us heredity is important. But his personal life tells us that nurture also is important from a young age. His life also demonstrates that a young person can grow up to be more devout and more scientific at the same time. Mendel's story is a welcome counterweight to Darwin's.

As we have seen, modern Western science has ancient Jewish and Christian roots. Now is a good time to help young people reconnect with those roots. The fruit of science and technology will be more likely to bring life and not death—life in the fullest sense—if we help young people to see simultaneously through eyes of science and eyes of the heart.

---

[10] Smith with Denton, *Soul Searching*, 90.

Our knowledge is incomplete. We do not possess a grand theory that unifies all the insights of science, let alone all the insights of science plus those of theology. But we have enough to go on; we can make progress. Above all, we have the person of Jesus in whom all things cohere, and we have the Holy Spirit as our ongoing Teacher. And in the pattern of Christ's personhood—two natures in union but not confusion, related but not conflated—we have a model for helping young people learn about faith and science. The two kinds of knowledge are distinct, as are the two natures of Jesus. Faith and science start from different premises, proceed by different methods, and arrive at different proofs. Yet they both pursue truth, they both seek to glimpse reality, and they both encounter mystery.

Therefore, we can teach young people to draw upon the insights of both ways of knowing. We don't need to steer them away from potential conflicts, for the place of severest conflict can become the place of deepest discovery. At the same time, we don't need to exasperate young people by placing undue obstacles in the path of faith. I have argued in this book that some readings of Genesis impede faith by taking an overly physical view of creation and by insisting that this view is a nonnegotiable cornerstone of biblical authority. Some parts of my arguments may turn out to be wrong. But the basic ideas about spiritual life and spiritual death set forth in this book have stood the test of time. These lessons need to be imparted to the next generation because a culture dominated by science and technology too easily occludes spiritual realities.

Faith and science need each other. Science and technology can draw upon the insights of faith to give ethical light to their endeavors and also to correct the reducing tendency of science. Even scientists want the universe to become a home. Meanwhile, a scientific sensibility can keep in check the exaggerating tendency of faith. Even the Bible instructs us to test and verify.

The pastor or parent who wants to engage youth in issues of faith and science instruction does not need to earn a PhD in physics or become a professional scientist. But some of their children may take precisely this path, and it will help them to know, growing up, that faith and science can be complementary and not conflicting routes to seeing God's reality. More than ever, the world needs Christians working in fields of science and technology. Humanity has more knowledge and power than ever before, yet the desire to be gods apart from God is just as dangerous today as it was in the Garden.

In the end, we all live by faith. The scientist trusts the universe has secrets to secrete, a hidden order waiting to be discovered. The believer trusts that God is a God of order and not confusion. But more than that—because life does bring confusion and senseless suffering—we teach our children well when we teach them to know and trust the love of God. This love is more vital than all human knowledge. If we know anything about Jesus, we know his love. And we come to trust, first as children and finally in our last days, that this love is able to transform all things, even turning death itself into a passage to fuller life.